T. W. Smith BA

Brodie's Notes on Charles

Great Expe

Pan Books London and Sydney

First published by James Brodie Ltd
This edition published 1976 by Pan Books Ltd
Cavaye Place, London SW10 9PG
16 17 18 19 20

ISBN 0 330 50016 3
Filmset in Great Britain by
Northumberland Press Ltd, Gateshead, Tyne and Wear
Printed and bound by
Richard Clay (The Chaucer Press) Ltd, Bungay, Suffolk

Contents

Page references in these Notes are to the Pan edition of *Great Expectations*, but references are usually given to particular chapters, so that the Notes may be used with any edition of the novel.

To the student

A close reading of the set book is the student's primary task. These Notes will help to increase your understanding and appreciation of the book and to stimulate *your own* thinking about it: *they are in no way intended as a substitute* for a thorough knowledge of the book.

The author and his work

Charles John Huffham Dickens was born on 7 February 1812 at Portsea, the eldest son of John and Elizabeth Dickens. His father was a clerk in the Navy Pay Office at Portsmouth, and was in many respects the prototype of the thriftless but perennially optimistic Mr Micawber in *David Copperfield*, the earlier chapters of which are based on Dickens's childhood. In 1814 he was transferred to London and in 1816 to Chatham, where the elder Dickens once told his son that, if he persevered, he might one day come to live in Gad's Hill Place (near Rochester), a prophecy that was to be fulfilled. In 1823 the family moved to Camden Town, London, and shortly afterwards, because of his financial difficulties, Mr Dickens was sent to the Marshalsea (debtors') Prison. During this time the boy was employed in a blacking factory, where his sensitive nature suffered more from the humiliation than any actual ill-treatment.

When his father was retired on a pension, Dickens was given two years of regular education, then entered the office of a Gray's Inn solicitor, where in eighteen months he acquired a knowledge of the law that he used with much effect in *Great Expectations*. He worked hard at shorthand, and in 1835 joined the staff of the *Morning Chronicle*, on which his father had already found a post. He was a parliamentary and descriptive reporter for seventeen years, travelling round the country by coach – remarkable for his keenness of observation and imaginative powers.

As a boy Dickens had read eagerly the works of Smollett, Fielding, Cervantes and other classical novelists; and as a young man he spent much time studying in the British Museum. In 1834 his first article was published; by 1836 his *Sketches by Boz* in the *Evening Chronicle* had drawn sufficient attention for him to publish them in two volumes. In the same year he married the daughter of the editor of the *Evening Chronicle*, Catherine Hogarth. The marriage was not a success, however, and they separated in 1858. He was next asked by Chapman and Hall to write the text to accompany a series of Cockney sporting plates, but a change of plan led to the formation of an imaginary club of sporting gentlemen, and *Pickwick Papers* began to appear in serial form in 1837. Their characteristic humour and pathos brought him instant fame. *Oliver Twist* and *Nicholas Nickleby* were soon being written simultaneously, and other novels appeared at the rate of about one a year. Publication in monthly parts made great demands upon him, and some of Dickens's work suffers from this pressure.

In 1842 Dickens crossed to America, where he was given a great reception. The satire in the *American Notes* (1842) and the novel *Martin Chuzzlewit* (1843), which dwelt on his American experiences, offended Americans for a time, but his second visit in 1867 was an even greater success.

In 1856 he purchased Gad's Hill Place, the dream of his childhood. He immediately began a series of improvements and did not permanently reside there till 1860. Surrounded by his large family, Dickens enjoyed being 'squire' to the villagers and played an active part in games and social festivities, especially at Christmas.

Dickens started a magazine of his own in 1859, *All the Year Round*, in which *Great Expectations* appeared in 1861. It was written during an interval between two reading tours, during which Dickens spent many pleasant hours striding along the country lanes round his home. A favourite walk was one of some five miles to the lonely churchyard of Cooling on the edge of the marshes between the rivers Thames and Medway. He frequently strolled the streets of Rochester where, in the Vines, stands the original of Satis House. The end of the story is said to have been composed on board a steamer on an excursion from London to the mouth of the Thames, in which Dickens spent one night at a riverside inn, The Ship and Lobster. The plot of *Great Expectations* was developed from a short story. In a letter to Forster, earlier in 1860, Dickens says:

> For a little piece I have been writing . . . such a very fine, new, and grotesque idea has opened upon me, that I begin to doubt whether I had not better cancel the little paper, and reserve the notion for a new book.

When quite young, Dickens had been taken to the theatre by a relative. This experience began a lifelong love of the stage. In those early days he used often to act as well as tell stories. In later years, he was for a time the manager of an amateur theatrical company. Dickens's greatest stage performance, however, was the reading of extracts from his books to enthusiastic audiences, here and in America (often for charity). The passages chosen were usually the most dramatic, and therefore the most exhausting; the work affected his health and he was reluctantly compelled to give it up.

Dickens's last work, *The Mystery of Edwin Drood* was interrupted in 1870 by his death, from a stroke, in his home at Gad's Hill Place. After his burial in Westminster Abbey, crowds filed reverently past his grave. His wide human sympathies, his spirited attacks on social evils, his vivid characterization and the entertainment he gave his readers, made Dickens the best-loved novelist of his century. He always had a large following among 'ordinary people'; that is still the secret of his popularity.

Further reading

A Reader's Guide to Charles Dickens, Philip Hobsbaum (Thames & Hudson)

The Dickens Encyclopedia, ed. Hayward (Routledge)

Dickens the Novelist, Sylvère Monod (University of Oklahoma Press) available UK

The Dickens Theatre, Robert Garis (OUP)

Plot and themes

Plot

As is often the case in Dickens's novels, *Great Expectations* has a very involved plot. The reader is presented with the results long before the causes, which often arrive as complete surprises; and there is usually much mystification. In the following outline the events of the story are arranged in chronological order.

A wealthy brewer named Havisham, who lives at Satis House in a market town not far from the south bank of the Thames estuary, has a daughter by his first wife and a son by the second. The son Arthur, is a wastrel, jealous that his half-sister has been left much more of his father's wealth than he has, teams up with a good-looking, well-educated intriguer called Compeyson. The latter wins Miss Havisham's affections to such an extent that she follows his advice implicitly and disregards that of her relations. When Compeyson swindles her of large sums of money and finally persuades her to buy Arthur's share in the brewery for an exorbitant amount, her cousin, Matthew Pocket, warns her against him and, for his pains, is ordered out of the house for good.

Miss Havisham was to be married to Compeyson, but he brutally breaks it off by letter on the wedding morning; he and Arthur, after spending their dishonest gains, take to a criminal life. Arthur dies in delirium, imagining his sister is putting a shroud on him; Compeyson has meanwhile enlisted Abel Magwitch to help him with his forgeries. Magwitch has been in and out of prison from youth, and at this time he has a baby daughter by a gipsy woman, Molly, who is standing trial for the murder of another woman of whom she was jealous.

The case for the defence is the first important one of a lawyer named Jaggers, who succeeds in getting her acquitted; Magwitch, however, goes into hiding at the time of the trial. Compeyson knows this and uses it as a hold over him. Both are eventually arrested for circulating stolen bank-notes, but in court Compeyson's counsel manages to put most of the blame on Magwitch, so that the latter's sentence is twice as heavy.

Both escape from the Hulks on the Thames in which they are serving their sentences, and Magwitch, intent on revenge, forfeits his chance of getting away by hunting down Compeyson on the marshes north of the town in which Miss Havisham lives. The result is that they are recaptured struggling together in a ditch, and Magwitch now receives a life sentence and is transported to Australia.

During his brief spell of liberty, Magwitch surprises a boy in a village churchyard on the edge of the marshes and frightens him into stealing for him a file and some food from his home. The boy, an orphan, lives with his harsh sister and her husband, Joe Gargery, the village blacksmith. The boy does as he is told by the convict without betraying him, and thus enables him to file away one of his leg-irons. Magwitch remembers it with gratitude, especially as the boy is about the same age as his own little girl, whom he believes to have been murdered by her wild mother.

Actually Jaggers had taken the mother permanently into his service immediately after the trial. When the lawyer is told by Miss Havisham that she wishes to adopt a little girl, he takes Magwitch's child, Estella, to Satis House, now a darkened, decaying household. Broken-hearted by her deceiver's letter, Miss Havisham has ordered everything, including the wedding-feast, to remain as it was, has stopped all the clocks and closed out the sunlight. She now lives as a recluse, and continues to wear her bridal dress. Miss Havisham rears the girl with the intention that she should avenge her patroness by breaking a man's heart when she grows up. One day, in pursuance of her grim purpose, she asks a tenant of hers, Pumblechook, for a boy to go and 'play' at her house. Pumblechook, a frequent visitor to the blacksmith's in the village by the marshes and 'uncle' to the boy, at once thinks of him and brings the news to Mrs Gargery. She sees the invitation as an opportunity for the boy to make his way in life and be off her hands.

Thus it is that Pip (short for Philip Pirrip), the hero of *Great Expectations*, comes on that 'one memorable day' to Satis, where he is mercilessly teased by Estella and made to feel ashamed of his commonness. Pip is frequently employed, for hours at a stretch, to wheel Miss Havisham round the two rooms in which she lives; eventually for this she gives Joe Gargery twenty-five guineas to pay for Pip's apprenticeship to the blacksmith's trade. The visits cease and not until a year later does Pip call at the big house, ostensibly to thank Miss Havisham, but in reality to see Estella, with whom the boy is inexplicably in love. Miss Havisham is there as usual, but Estella has gone to a finishing school in France, and the boy comes away more dissatisfied than ever with the humbleness of his own home surroundings. When he gets back home, Pip finds that his sister has been murderously attacked (by Orlick, Joe's assistant); she remains an invalid till her death, and Biddy, a true-hearted village girl, who first helped Pip to learn his letters, comes to the forge to take charge.

Three years later, Jaggers is commissioned by Magwitch, who has made a fortune by sheep-rearing in New South Wales, to give the blacksmith's boy the education of a gentleman, to fit him to inherit his wealth. The name of Pip's benefactor is to be kept a secret till he chooses to reveal it himself in person. Pip assumes that the anonymous author of his 'Great Expectations' is Miss Havisham, and that Estella also is destined to be his. He goes to London, where he studies under Matthew Pocket at Hammersmith, and lives in rooms in town with Herbert, Pocket's son, whom he first met as a boy and with whom he has had a fight at Satis House. Herbert is employed in an office with very poor prospects. The two young men now, however, become friends for life. Pip also forms a close acquaintanceship with Wemmick, Jaggers's clerk, who, out of office hours, is to prove of the greatest assistance to him.

One day Joe comes to London with a message from Miss Havisham that Estella has returned to Satis and wishes to see Pip. His youthful love for the intended breaker of his heart is now intensified by her beauty as a young woman, but she warns him that all tenderness has been bred out of her by Miss Havisham. Before long she comes to reside with a family at Richmond who introduce her to society; Pip is required by Miss Havisham to accompany Estella on social engagements, a duty which proves more of a torture than a pleasure.

Since his change of fortune Pip has shamefacedly avoided his humble relations at the forge, and his remorse for neglecting Joe, the devotedly faithful companion of his childhood, is deepened after being suddenly called home to the funeral of his sister. The shallowness of his promise to go back oftener is unmasked by the shrewd but tactful Biddy. Back in London, Pip gains some happiness by secretly negotiating a partnership for Herbert with some of his money. He is, however, dismayed to find Estella encouraging the advances of a boorish fellow called Drummle, whom he had first met studying under Matthew Pocket (who largely depended for his livelihood on private tutoring). Pip finds little consolation in Estella's generous confession that she wishes to spare him, alone of all men, the unhappiness of becoming her victim.

When Pip is twenty-three, the blow falls which shatters all his dreams. Magwitch, who has returned from Australia at the risk of his life in order to see the young 'gentleman' he has created, makes himself known to Pip in his rooms at the Temple. He has assumed the name of 'Provis', and Pip decides to call him his uncle. Unknown to them, the ex-convict's movements have already been spied on by Orlick, who holds Pip responsible for his discharge from the Havisham household where he had been employed as a porter. He therefore seeks to avenge himself. Pip and Herbert decide that Magwitch must be taken abroad again, and, if necessary, that Pip should accompany him. Before any further steps are taken, Pip visits Satis and learns that Estella is to be married to Drummle – to spare him.

On his return to London, Pip finds a note from Wemmick warning him not to go to his rooms; next day he sees the clerk at his house in the suburbs and is told that he is being watched. 'Provis' is immediately taken downriver to stay in the same house as Herbert's fiancée and her father, and Pip and Herbert start rowing regularly, in preparation for the day when they might row from Magwitch's hide-out to an outward-bound steamer, for Pip and his ex-convict benefactor to get on board and out of the country.

Some weeks pass in this way when Pip is once more summoned by Miss Havisham. She first gives him a cheque for £900, in response to an earlier appeal by him for assistance (which he could no longer give, having made up his mind not to touch Magwitch's money) in completing the partnership for Herbert. Miss Havisham then asks for, and receives his forgiveness for the hard-hearted trick she has played on his affections. He is about to leave after a last tour of the grounds in which he had once walked with Estella, when the recurrence of a boyhood vision of Miss Havisham hanging from a beam prompts him to return upstairs. Pip finds Miss Havisham with her clothes alight but manages to smother the flames though suffering burns himself. Leaving her unconscious in the care of a surgeon and giving instructions that Estella should be sent for, Pip returns to London, where his burns are carefully dressed by Herbert.

Herbert is soon full of his business prospects; the cheque enables a new branch to be opened in the East which Herbert is to go out and take charge of. Then a note from Wemmick warns them to get Magwitch away in two days' time. The same day an anonymous note from Orlick referring to his 'Uncle Provis' entices Pip to a lonely part of the marshes, where he narrowly escapes being murdered by Orlick. Herbert had found the note and followed him, and arrives just in time. After a day's rest they row downriver with another friend, pick up Magwitch and spend the night at a lonely riverside inn, where they learn of a mysterious boat hovering in the neighbourhood.

Next morning they are about to board a Hamburg steamer when the mystery boat appears and they are called on by officers, who have a heavily muffled informer with them, to surrender Magwitch as a returned convict. The police boat draws alongside as the steamer is bearing down upon them, and at the moment of impact Pip's boat is run down. Magwitch seizes and unmasks the informer, who proves to be Compeyson. Pip and his friends are rescued, but the two convicts disappear, struggling. Compeyson does not come to the surface again, while Magwitch is picked up and taken to prison. There, Magwitch is placed in the infirmary because of his injuries from the paddle-steamer. Pip visits him regularly; he no longer has anything to expect from his benefactor and is now truly devoted to him. In the interval before the trial, he sees Wemmick happily married. At the next Sessions, Magwitch is duly condemned to death, but he dies before the day of execution, not, however, before Pip tells him that his daughter has grown into a beautiful woman and that he himself is in love with her.

The strain of events brings on a fever, from which Pip recovers, after some weeks, to find Joe Gargery, his faithful but neglected friend, by his bedside, having been his constant nurse through his illness. When Pip is restored to health Joe tactfully leaves for home early one morning, leaving a note and a receipt for a debt Pip had incurred and was unable to settle. Three days later Pip follows, having made up his mind to live at the forge and to ask Biddy to overlook the past and marry him. He arrives to find Biddy just married to Joe. After a farewell to his oldest friends and the familiar surroundings of his youth, he accepts Herbert's offer of a clerkship in the office in the East.

Eleven years later, now a partner in the firm, Pip returns to England and finds Joe and Biddy happy with their growing family. Visiting the site of Satis House, which has been pulled down, he encounters Estella, also paying it a last farewell. She has been ill-treated by Drummle, before separating from him, but is now freed by his death.

Her heart has been changed by her sufferings, and she asks Pip's forgiveness. Together they leave the ruins of the strange house in which they had first met, never to part again.

Themes

Few novelists have written books with such clarity of purpose behind them as Dickens. His attacks on social evils, such as the Poor Law in *Oliver Twist*, the Court of Chancery in *Bleak House*, imprisonment for debt in *David Copperfield*, and the Yorkshire schools in *Nicholas Nickleby*, led in some cases to reforms. Whereas in earlier novels this moral purpose is apt to be obtruded on the reader, it is not so in *Great Expectations*. Here the story comes a long way first, and the lessons to be drawn from it are only to be inferred.

First of these is *the influence of money on human character*. It pervades the book. The Pockets (with the exception of Matthew and his family) greedily hope to benefit from Miss Havisham's will, and that lady maliciously enjoys making them envious of Pip, who in reality is not the favoured one. Pip himself, having seen his small earnings as a boy regularly confiscated, has his head turned by unexpected affluence and soon leads not only himself but Herbert into serious debt. A most demoralizing spectacle to Pip is the complete change of manner on the part of the tradesmen, Trabb and Pumblechook. That money can be put to a good purpose is demonstrated by Miss Havisham's payment of Pip's apprenticeship fees; the buying of Herbert's partnership; and the bequest to Matthew that followed Pip's praise of him. Magwitch's use of his wealth was an act of devotion, and Pip's decision to forego it, though at first made on snobbish grounds, is continued in a spirit of remorseful sacrifice.

Hardly less important is *the hollowness of a false gentility*. In this respect Pip is the example by which to take warning. A pretty girl, reared in better circumstances, first makes him painfully aware of his own coarseness and the humble condition in which he lives. For her sake he longs to become a 'gentleman', and when he is so fortunate as to be able to live like one, wearing the right clothes, behaving correctly at table and eventually escorting the pretty girl on a round of social activities, he shamefully neglects the honest blacksmith who is his truest friend. Indeed, Pip is extremely embarrassed by Joe's uncouth behaviour in the presence of people like Herbert and Miss Havisham.

It is difficult to estimate just how snobbish Pip is, since we are given only his own mental reactions; the bitter humiliation inflicted on him by Trabb's Boy may have been due to some conceit in his bearing, or it may have been only a mischievous urchin's readiness to poke fun at the smartly dressed. What we do know is that, by the irony of fate, Pip rose above his station, thanks to the whim of a convict of the coarsest type, and that, when his career was wrecked, he was patiently nursed back to health by the awkward, inarticulate Joe, whom he had avoided while he was a man of fashion. Both of these had a pride of their own and they knew their own shortcomings only too well to attempt any kind of pretence. However, they had a depth of feeling that exceeded anything of which Pip was capable; and their affection for him surpassed in warmth and loyalty the romantic admiration Pip felt for Estella.

The character most worthy of admiration is, of course, Joe Gargery, and it is therefore quite probable that Dickens's positive purpose, as distinct from the negative ones just described – the deceptive lure of money and the fascination of a false gentility – was to show wherein true gentlemanliness lies. Lacking in birth and breeding, the village blacksmith is loyal, considerate, patient, tactful and forgiving, in contrast with his young apprentice who, though a boy of naturally kind instincts, is betrayed by his ambition to appear a gentleman into selfishness, meanness, moral cowardice and all the outward trappings of snobbery.

Setting and atmosphere

Setting

Period

Without suggesting that Dickens had any particular years in mind (the book is quite devoid of dates), we can place the events of the story fairly accurately by means of 'internal evidence'. Pip was twenty-three when he practised 'shooting' Old London Bridge, which was demolished in 1831, after the opening of the new bridge; he was just under twenty-one when, escorting Estella one night, he came into the glare of gas, not used for street illumination before 1827. These two references would make the year of his birth approximately 1807, five years before that of his creator: in writing the novel, Dickens, as well as Pip, would be looking back on his youth.

Among other details may be noted Orlick's use of the old flint, steel and tinder-box, superseded in 1837 by matches (called 'lucifer matches' at the time); Pip's thought of adding a balloon to his fictitious tale of wonders at Satis House (ballooning became very popular in the 1820s); the steam-traffic on the Thames (started in 1816) 'far below its present extent', and watermen's boats (later eliminated by land transport) 'far more numerous'. An interesting allusion is the comparison of Pip, in his fear of the theft of the pie being found out, moving the table to 'a medium of the present day'; as Spiritualism did not reach Britain till 1852, Pip must have been writing his memoirs at the age of at least forty-five.

There are a limited number of minor social features of the early nineteenth century, such as musical glasses, waxworks at fairs, tar-water and rushlights, but nothing of the economic distress and political upheavals of the time. The novel, beginning in the Napoleonic wars and ending in the years of Parliamentary reform, moves in a fantastic little world of its own, its only contact with outside affairs lying in the grim sphere of law-court and prison. Pip's upbringing was to be associated with crime, and no other factors must be allowed to interfere with this conception.

Of crime and its detection and punishment we are given vividly realistic pictures. Robberies were common, sentences ferocious and prisons horrible institutions. At the beginning of the century the penalty for over 150 offences was death by hanging, which was a public spectacle. The last public hanging in Britain was not until 1868.) Magwitch was condemned with thirty-one others; these others would meet their fates early in the morning and be cut down before nine o'clock. On the marshes stood one of those gibbets on which malefactors were left hanging, and condemned men were to be encountered, manacled and fettered, among one's fellow-travellers on public coaches. Until the establishment of a regular police force in 1829, police work was mainly done by soldiers, while special investigations were entrusted to those 'extinct red-waist-coated police', the Bow Street runners, satirized by Dickens (as their successors have been in modern detective fiction) for absurd blunders, like suspecting Joe of the murder of his wife!

Locality

In his last novels Dickens returned to his own district, the neighbourhood of Rochester, and, though no names in this Kentish region are given (in contrast with London, which is mapped out in detail), there is no doubt about the localities concerned.

The marshes In the tongue of land lying between the estuaries of the Thames and the Medway, the Cooling and Cliffe Marshes stretch from the villages of the same names northwards to the bank of the Thames. Their flatness and 'bleak stillness' throw into relief the beacon (the Shorne Mead Light) and the old Battery (probably Shorne Mead). About 3 km (2 miles) downriver would be the cement works near which Pip is nearly murdered. Round Lower Hope Point a path skirts the edge of the Thames leading to the landing stage where the convicts were taken back to the Hulks. For a long time after Pip's day seven old Hulks were moored off-shore and used as powder magazines. The marshes were crossed by sluices, each with its miniature windmill and muddy sluice-gate; there were reeds and rushes in the swampy parts, while cattle were pastured on the expanse of grass.

The village Some 8 km (5 miles) north of Rochester is the lonely churchyard of Cooling, and among its quaint gravestones can be seen the lozenges, so humorously treated in the first page of the book. In Pip's time it was overgrown with nettles and brambles; the tower had a steeple and weathercock; between it and the sea was the horizontal line of the marshes, across which would sweep the wild sea wind. About 3 km (1 mile) from the marshes was the forge, with the wooden cottage of the blacksmith. Nearby was the 'Three Jolly Bargemen' and at the end of the lane the signpost, at one time a ghostly finger hovering in the mist, at another the last link with home.

The town The 'Blue Boar' has been identified with the 'Bull Hotel', celebrated in *Pickwick Papers*, and Satis House with Restoration House in the Vines, Rochester (originally the Monks' Vineyard). However, the name was taken from another mansion, close to the Castle and so called because, when Queen Elizabeth was asked by her host, after he had entertained her there for one night, whether her accommodation had been satisfactory, she is said to have replied, 'Satis'!

In Chapter 49 Pip refers to the ruins of the monks' refectories and gardens, the rooks hovering about the cathedral tower and the trees of the ancient priory, the sounds of the cathedral bells and the solemn peal of the organ. In Chapter 29 he describes the exterior of the house with its 'seared red brick walls, blocked windows, and strong green ivy clasping even the stacks of chimneys with its twigs and tendons' (p.223). Outside was a wilderness of a garden and a disused brewery, strewn with empty casks; inside a succession of dark passages, leading to the two rooms, where, lit by candles in sconces high up on the walls, the half-mad, witchlike Miss Havisham, surrounded by the decaying remnants of the wedding-feast, tormented her relatives, gloated over Estella's beauty and fed herself with scraps at midnight.

In the High Street of the 'quiet old town' stood not only Pumblechook's corn and seed shop and Trabb's, the tailor's, but the premises of numerous tradesmen, among whom business was so sluggish that they spent much of their time watching each other.

The capital The journey to London by stage-coach took five hours, the terminus being the Cross Keys in Wood Street, Cheapside. Pip was awed by the capital's immensity, but disgusted by its ugliness and dirt. After a short acquaintance with the filth of Smithfield and the grimness of Newgate Prison, where he is shown the gallows and whipping-post, Pip finds himself billeted in Barnard's Inn, 'the dingiest collection of shabby buildings ever squeezed together in a rank corner as a club for Tom-cats', and concludes that London is 'decidedly over-rated'.

Pip is destined to see more of Newgate. His tour of the cells with Wemmick is described in Chapter 32. The trial scene, in which the thirty-two capital sentences were pronounced together, is given in Chapter 56. In 1864, shortly before these executions ceased to be public spectacles, a crowd of fifty thousand saw a murderer hanged, barrels of beer being provided for the occasion. The gallows stood very close to the present entrance to the Central Criminal Court in Old Bailey.

The Temple, to which Pip and Herbert migrated from Barnard's Inn, was then rather lonely and exposed to the wind off the river. Hammersmith, where the eccentric Pockets lived, and Richmond, the home of the aristocratic Brandleys, were then separated from London by miles of country road. South of the Thames was the suburb of Walworth and the 'Castle' of Wemmick. Jaggers lived in Gerrard Street, Soho. Apart from Herbert's humble place of employment, very little is seen of the background of teeming city life by which Pip is surrounded for some four years – lamplighters, a chop-house, a lodging-house and the theatre.

The river As the ebb tide flowed past the Temple, Herbert thought of it as carrying everything to his beloved Clara at Chinks's Basin; Pip dreaded to think that somewhere on its surface Magwitch's pursuers were hastening to arrest him. Pip's journeys by river afford little glimpses of the great waterway down which Magwitch was transported to Australia, to return years later, wealthy but still a convict, and on which, not only changed in heart himself but having wrought a change of heart in the boy he had made into a gentleman, he met his fate.

On that last ill-starred expedition, the three young men cast off from Temple Stairs, thread their way through a maze of small craft, passing Old London Bridge, Billingsgate with its oyster-boats and Dutch vessels and the Tower with its Traitor's Gate, observe the outward-bound steamers and reach Mill Pond Stairs. As the drama approaches its climax, and the anxious crew of the rowing-boat scan the shipping and the shores for signs of danger, the descriptive part of the narrative becomes more detailed: cables and hawsers, buoys and ships' figure-heads, scum and flotsam, the mingled noises of hammers, sawmills, pumps, capstans and shouting. After Gravesend they pass the floating Custom House, emigrant ships and troop transports, and come to the marshy stretches where decrepit landing-stages, dilapidated light-houses and rows of stakes stick up out of the mud and slime. Stealing past mysterious creeks they put up at a dirty, suspicious-looking tavern, where the serving man gets his clothes from the bodies of the drowned.

The scenes amidst which Pip waits for his expectations to be realized are uniformly depressing, brightened, however, by the cheerful personalities of Herbert Pocket and Wemmick. On the other hand, those social occasions at which Pip has been destined by his unknown benefactor to play a conspicuous part are blighted by the disagreeable Drummle and the tantalizing relationship with Estella.

Atmosphere

After a series of rather gloomy novels (*Bleak House*, *Hard Times* and *Little Dorrit*) Dickens recovered some of his earlier high spirits and playful humour in *Great Expectations*. Though, as we have seen, there is still plenty of bleakness and hardness, the reader is once more regularly amused by the irresistibly comic writing; and deeply moved by two of the author's greatest creations from humble life: Joe Gargery and Abel Magwitch. There is, too, an underlying vein of gently cynical fun, possibly at the expense of himself: in the 'Castle', where the drawbridge and bower may be a tilt at his own 'vanities' at Gad's Hill Place, with its underground passage to the Swiss chalet in 'The Wilderness' on the other side of the road; in Pip's array of books, from which he read to Magwitch 'foreign languages wot I don't understand'; in Wopsle's love of recitation which led him to a stage career in which he played many parts.

There is considerable play of light and shadow symbolizing the bright prospects and the hidden scheming that shape the story. Predominant are the mists of the marshes, in the half-lights of which familiar objects loom up like phantoms; when the mists rise to give way to sunlight, they seem to reveal to Pip what life offers him: on his first journey to London, the world lies spread before him; on his return from his sister's funeral, the plain truth that years are to pass before he visits his old home again; at his final meeting with Estella, the knowledge that he will never be parted from her again. More frequent than the sunshine in which Pip talks with Biddy or Herbert is the presence of artificial light: the candles in Satis, the new gas-lamps in the London streets lit at dusk by an army of lamplighters, the old-fashioned rushlight in the Hummums, the reading-lamp with which

Pip first receives 'Provis', the candle held up by Orlick while he gloats over his helpless 'enemy'.

The use of sounds is also effective, particularly the slight noises heard in an oppressive stillness: the rasping of a file in the eerie quiet of the marshes, the mice behind the panels of Satis, the nocturnal creakings in the Hummums, the mysterious ripples as the fugitives creep down-river in the dark.

Death figures prominently in Dickens's novels, and few of its aspects are missing from this book, from the gravestones with whose help Pip started learning his letters, to the deathbed of Magwitch. There is also the shock of his sister's death, followed by the farcical spectacle of the funeral in full mourning; Miss Havisham's death from injuries by fire and her former lover's death by drowning; Pip's vivid recollections of his past life as he watches his would-be murderer's movements; and in the background the shadow of the gallows, which the ex-convict cheated in the end.

Home life is equally prominent. There are two real homes: firstly, the forge, after Mrs Gargery's bitter tongue has been put to silence. From it Pip is separated by the influence of money and the attraction of Estella, but it retains its hold on his affections, for, before leaving for the East, he has to say goodbye to his old bedroom under the roof and to the signpost at the end of the lane. It has been 'sanctified' for him by Joe's character. And secondly, the 'Castle', on which its owner lavishes his ingenuity. Here the 'Walworth sentiment' creates an atmosphere far removed from that of Jaggers's office and finds its supreme expression in Wemmick's tender and patient care of the Aged Parent.

The cloak of secrecy casts its folds over many parts. Pip himself is a repository of secrets, from the opening chapter, when he becomes the unwilling accomplice of a runaway convict, to the tracking down of Estella's parentage. His own career is a secret, and in secret he starts Herbert on his career. Infinite precautions are taken in Jaggers's office to prevent secrets from leaking out, and the habit is comically maintained by Wemmick at his marriage, the wedding ceremony being disguised as a fishing expedition. Equally great precautions are taken by Pip and Herbert in their attempt to prevent Magwitch's arrest; the movements which lead to his recognition and tracking down are wrapped in mystery.

Dickens's novels are full of people with expectations (of whom

Micawber in *David Copperfield* is the best-known example), and in them there is frequent expectation of good and frequent dread of evil. Most of Pip's time is spent in expectation of realizing his fortune or in dread of exposure; Herbert 'looked about him' for an opportunity of making 'Capital'; the Pockets (except those at Hammersmith) toady to Miss Havisham in expectation of benefiting from her will; that lady herself lives for the day when Estella will work out her scheme of revenge on the male sex.

Events, in fiction as well as in life, turn out differently from what is anticipated and come often as surprises when least expected. Pip longs to be a gentleman and fit for Estella's company when suddenly he is spirited into fashionable life, only to find a gulf between him and the object of his devotion; when Magwitch climbs the stairs with his bulging pocketbook, Pip prefers poverty to his fortune; Herbert's opportunity is found for him by his friend; the Pockets, jealous of the wrong person, find themselves passed over in favour of the one member of their family who has not toadied; Miss Havisham suffers agonies of remorse at the moment of her triumph.

Dickens was apt to stretch coincidence to the limit of the incredible: that Miss Havisham and Magwitch should employ the same lawyer is just plausible, but Pip's meeting with Estella in the ruins of Satis reads too much like a fairy tale.

Structure and style

Structure

In this novel Dickens returned to the autobiographical method of *David Copperfield*; like his better-known prototype, Pip recounts the cruel circumstances of his boyhood and his heart-searching as a young man. The book has been called a 'novel without a hero', but this is hardly true in the literary sense, as Pip is the central character in all the major incidents, and rather unfair in the moral sense, since, while he plays mainly a passive part waiting on events to shape his career, he is not devoid of noble instincts and generous resolves.

The fantastic story of Miss Havisham is framed in the far more convincing setting of the village on the edge of the marshes. The story begins and ends at the blacksmith's forge, for Pip's reunion with Estella is no more than an epilogue. The contrast between the occupants of the big brick mansion and those of the humble wooden cottage is the starting point of Pip's false pilgrimage after gentility; when he returns years later, only the site of Satis House remains, but a happy little family is growing up at the smithy.

Pip is not only disappointed, but deceived. His destiny was decided for him not by an eccentric patroness, but by a transported convict toiling in the lonely sheep pastures of New South Wales. The taint of prison and crime which clung to him after that first encounter in the churchyard, and from which he sought to escape as from the 'commonness' of his upbringing, return with overwhelming force to shatter his dreams.

The whole development, in fact, is based on the opening chapters: the memory of Pip leads to Magwitch's reformation and his determination later to make the boy's fortune. The ex-convict is not to know that his desire to remain anonymous until he can see his 'gentleman' for himself leads Pip into believing that he is being made fit by Miss Havisham to marry Estella, a belief to which the young man clings even while he knows that Estella has been trained to victimize those who fall in love with her. Thus we have the curious position that while the beauty of Magwitch's daughter is being used by Miss Havisham to break Pip's heart, the wealth of the father is being lavished on him because he has reminded the tough old gaol-bird of the very same daughter; further, Pip shrinks from Magwitch because of the beauty and breeding he associates with Magwitch's daughter! The reader can hardly ask for anything more involved. Estella, whom Pip loved first and last, is the instrument on the one hand of grotesque spite towards him and, on the other, of grotesque generosity.

In these days it is difficult to think in terms of monthly magazine parts, but that was the way in which the majority of Dickens's novels appeared. It was a method which imposed a strain on the author, especially on one so devoted to the interests of his reading public as Dickens, and the results are often to be seen in hasty composition, unreal incidents, superfluous characters and lapses in style. It seems sometimes as if Dickens feels bound to provide both humour and pathos in a single instalment. That alternation is noticeable in *Great Expectations*: the farcical encounter with Drummle comes between Magwitch's life history and Pip's declaration of love to Estella; Wemmick's wedding between the arrest of Magwitch and his trial. Pip's escape from the clutches of Orlick is a piece of unnecessary melodrama, calculated perhaps to relieve the tension of waiting for the moment of getting 'Provis' on board an outward-bound steamer.

The book is divided into three 'stages': the first, Chapters 1–19, ends with Pip's departure for London to be educated as a gentleman; the second, Chapters 20–39, ends with the appearance of his real benefactor; the third, Chapters 40–58, ends with Pip's departure for the East; and the final chapter effects a change in the ending that had been suggested by Dickens's friend, Bulwer Lytton. 'I have no doubt,' the author wrote, 'the story will be the more acceptable through the alteration.'

This was certainly a concession to the feelings of his readers; it would have been an artistic ending for Pip to lose Estella, but it would have been very unpopular. As it is, it is a sad little reunion, and vaguely inconclusive. The film version of the novel made quite certain of the matter by bringing them together immediately after Pip's recovery and sparing them eleven years of separation. The title logically suggests 'Great Disappointments', but our sympathy with the blacksmith's boy, whose life, moral as well as material, has been moulded by his expectations, requires an ending which satisfies our emotion rather than our reason.

There is, too, enough of tragedy in the fate of Magwitch. The old man dies happy in the thought of his boy enjoying his wealth and loving his daughter; it would have been too much for the reader that both of these beliefs should be illusions. The scenes in which Magwitch is concerned are the most vivid in the book, and Dickens was at his best in working up to a climax like the final capture of the ex-convict.

The period between the announcement of Pip's expectations and their collapse is filled by Dickens with an array of characters and a succession of scenes in which his creative fancy had full play. The opening and closing chapters are, on the other hand, intensely dramatic. A noteworthy feature is the way in which the chief villain of the book is seen only by glimpses, crouching in a ditch, crouching in a theatre audience or crouching in a boat; we see the results of his scheming, but he works out of sight most of the time. The manner of his death is a well-deserved punishment for the misery he had brought upon others.

Style

The autobiographical novel has its advantages – and its limitations. When it is told by one who has experienced and has 'remembered' the adventures, a greater sense of reality is given to the story than could be achieved by the impersonal approach from outside. At the same time, much that the reader would like to know, particularly the thoughts and feelings of the other characters, hidden as they must be from the hero, can only be supplied by an 'omniscient' author.

The chief characteristics of Dickens's prose are its simplicity, its emotional quality and its frequent use of humorous turns of phrase. He wrote with huge enjoyment, if sometimes under considerable strain. In a jovial mood he would exaggerate to the limit; in sad moments he could achieve the tenderest pathos with the simplest expression. His material did not call for the subtle arts of the fine writer; at his best he used pure English in vigorous and racy narrative and perfect clarity of sentence structure. There are however, occasions, only too often, when he descended to unbelievable bathos, cheap jokes and maudlin sentiment.

Dickens's literary training was imperfect – in fact he owed more to his journalistic experience than to other authors, of whom Fielding and Smollett influenced him most – but he strove hard to improve his style. Largely self-educated, he has faults and mannerisms that offend the purist; nevertheless, they are swallowed up in the zest with which he arrests the reader's attention, and in the wealth of detail and colour with which he invests his characters and incidents. He started his regular public readings in 1853, and his later novels, including *Great Expectations*, may well have been written, in places, with an eye on future declamation. The book is certainly sprinkled with passages that lend themselves to recitation, and with character sketches that lend themselves to humorous impersonation.

As if to counterbalance the grim circumstances and dismal atmosphere of much of the story, humorous treatment is much more frequent than pathos: Pip and Herbert making memoranda of their debts; Wopsle's stage performances; and Wemmick's wedding, provide comic interludes. Frequently these incidents are strained to the limits of the farcical: the Pocket baby and the nutcrackers; Pumblechook shaking hands; Trabb's Boy mocking Pip; Wemmick's courting; Drummle's driving; and the funeral procession. The description of Jaggers in court; 'Mr Waldengarver' as Hamlet; and the waiter providing 'tea' for Pip and Estella, are typical examples of Dickens's humour. Joe writing a letter is strongly reminiscent of Sam Weller in *Pickwick Papers*.

There is pathos in Pip's departures from home and in the death of Magwitch. Pip, whose tears soon dry after the signpost has been left behind; or when Joe, forgotten in thoughts of Estella, is the cause of tears shed by others: Joe when parting with him, Miss Havisham when asking his forgiveness, Estella when recollecting many years later how she had first rejected his love, Magwitch at his first cold welcome.

There are occasional satirical touches: Mr Pocket's lectures on domestic economy; Mrs Pocket's father being knighted for composing the address at the laying of a foundation stone by Royalty; the greasy condition of a fashionable eating-house; the gentility of brewing as compared with baking; the police suspecting Joe of the assault on his wife; the dark state of his wife's mind after the attack, in finding no more meaning in the simplest words than in an election cry!

Dickens excels in the apt phrase: the windows in Barnard's Inn consisting of 'dilapidated blind and curtain, crippled flower-pot, cracked glass, dusty decay, and miserable makeshift'; the candles at Satis that 'faintly troubled its darkness'; Matthew Pocket wondering vaguely why his children had not been 'billeted by Nature on somebody else'. Simile is frequently used to portray some aspect of a character's appearance: the newly-wed Mrs Wemmick being embraced like a 'cello; Orlick like a human doormouse in the porter's room at Satis; Joe and Pip crossing their fingers like the legs of Crusaders' effigies (probably seen by Pip in the Temple Church); Joe in his Sunday clothes like a 'scarecrow in good circumstances'; the boy Pip being goaded by the grown-ups 'like an unfortunate little bull in a Spanish arena'.

Some of these expressions are passed off as Pip's 'homely thoughts', like the neglected box-tree resembling a pudding that has stuck to the saucepan and got burnt. A certain amount of artificial liveliness is obtained by the personification of inanimate objects: the houses peeping in through Jaggers's skylight; the flower-seeds pining in Pumblechook's packets as if in gaol; the bellows in Joe's forge roaring after the runaway convicts. To Pip's imaginative mind animal life assumes human attitudes: the once accusing cattle show a new respect for a young man of fortune; the rooks warn him of Estella's departure from Satis; and in the old house are the agitated spiders and aldermanic beetles.

There are several passages of sordidly realistic detail: the manacled convicts with their flavour of 'bread-poultice, baize, rope-yarn and hearth-stone'; the depressing hotel room in which Pip and Estella have tea; the infested lodging-house where Pip spends the night away from his rooms; the river surface on the way to Gravesend. Occasionally the smallest details, particularly of furnishing, are obtruded on our notice, as if there could not be enough true-to-life background: the china poodles on Mrs Joe's parlour mantelshelf; the umbrella over the 'Stinger'; the formally clipped trees at Richmond; the gravy stains on tavern tablecloths. Descriptions are made clear to the reader by an author's choice of *significant* detail (not by the *amount* of detail, which may only obscure the impression).

The novel opens among tombstones, in marsh country – a 'dark flat wilderness beyond the churchyard, intersected with dykes and mounds and gates', down by the river – a 'low, leaden line', on a *raw* afternoon of rushing wind, in a 'bleak place overgrown with nettles'. Sympathetic background is an old device, harmonizing the weather and the situation with events in the story, at once intensifying the atmosphere and broadening it, as if not only the few people in the story were affected, but the whole universe. Ruskin condemned this crediting of Nature with human emotions (so that Nature appears to sympathize with human affairs) as the 'pathetic fallacy'. It can, of course, be overplayed, and Ruskin characterized the 'pathetic fallacy' as 'a *falseness* in . . . impressions of external things'. Let Ruskin say what he will, this 'falseness' is found in the tragedies of Shakespeare, the novels of Hardy and the poems of Wordsworth – to mention only a few.

In *Great Expectations* the weather and the natural background become symbols. The novel closes as the moon begins to rise, 'the silvery mist was touched with the first rays of the moonlight . . . I took her hand in mine, and we went out of the ruined place; and, as the morning mists had risen long ago when I first left the forge [end of Chapter 19], so, the evening mists were rising now, and in all the broad expanse of tranquil light they showed to me, I saw no shadow of another parting from her.' The rising of the evening mists on a moonlit night symbolizes the beginning of a quietly happy future after the turbulent past. It must be admitted that Dickens made more use of sympathetic background for dismal scenes than for happy ones. For instance, the weather on Wemmick's marriage morning is not even mentioned. In a similar way *objects* seem to absorb the atmosphere and the feeling of the beholder, as the expression of 'the two ghastly casts on the shelf' in Jaggers's office 'was as if they were making a stupid apoplectic attempt to attend to the conversation'.

There are numerous examples of Dickens's mannerisms. Humorous periphrasis, the most characteristic of them all, is scattered throughout the book: 'Long after these constitutional powers had dispersed' for the departure of the constables from the forge; 'those obscure corners of pork of which the pig, when living, had had the least reason to be vain' for the scraps given to Pip; Mr Wopsle's great-aunt's pupils emerging after school uttering 'shrieks of intellectual victory'. This habit may have derived from the author's early experience of newspapers – a typical specimen of 'journalese' is Pumblechook's 'puff' in Chapter 28.

Sometimes this roundabout way of saying things is overdone, as in 'conquered a confirmed habit of living' for 'died'; perhaps Wemmick's caution may excuse such a roundabout expression as 'a certain part of the world where a good many people go, not always in gratification of their own inclinations, and not quite irrespective of the government', yet there seems no good reason why, in private conversation, he should not have said 'Australia', unless it be Dickens's own 'confirmed habit' of long-winded allusions! A similar and quite effective trick is the accumulation of synonyms: 'The bill paid, and the waiter remembered, and the ostler not forgotten, and the chambermaid taken into consideration – in a word, the whole house bribed into a state of contempt and animosity, and Estella's purse much lightened.' Critical comment, worthy of a modern purist, is expended on Orlick's use of 'jiggered' in Chapter 17 and in Joe's phrase, 'a *cool* four thousand' in Chapter 57.

Other kinds of emphasis are seen in simple repetition: 'mud, mud, mud, deep in all the streets'; 'I could never, never, never, undo what I had done.' And groups of four closely associated words: Pip found London 'ugly, crooked, narrow and dirty' and the interior of Newgate 'frouzy, ugly, disorderly and depressing'; he turned with disgust from Smithfield 'asmear with filth and fat and blood and foam'. When he first saw Magwitch, the convict 'limped and shivered, and glared and growled'; another convict summed up life in the Hulks as 'mudbank, mist, swamp and work: work, swamp, mist and mudbank'. There are even larger groups of words – Mrs Joe's merciless washing of Pip: 'I was soaped and kneaded, and towelled, and thumped, and harrowed, and rasped'; Wopsle's idea of educating Pip by declaiming dramatic passages at him, with appropriate gestures, so that Pip was 'contradicted and embraced and wept over and bullied and clutched and stabbed and knocked about in a variety of ways'. And, of course, there is exaggeration: Pip seeing 'miles of open country' through Mr Hubble's legs, or the shopkeepers in town engaged in watching each other, like links in a chain.

Dickens is sometimes guilty of a clumsy conceit: the various rotten smells in Barnard's Inn suggesting to Pip that he should 'Try Barnard's Mixture'; those who rumpled Pip's hair described as taking 'ophthalmic steps' to patronize him; and the extraordinary confirmation that Wopsle had sat down several times in the wet by the removal of his coat – whereupon 'the circumstantial evidence on his trousers would have hanged him if it had been a capital offence'. Pip's confused state of mind may possibly excuse a mixed metaphor, when he described Trabb's Boy as 'an invulnerable and dodging serpent who, when chased into a corner, flew out again between his captor's legs, scornfully yelping'. Dickens's faults, however, have been truly described as 'the excess of his virtues,' and we overlook gross exaggeration under the stimulus of his vigorous narrative powers.

Apart from Wopsle's recitations, there are no literary allusions. An eastern fable provides an elaborate analogy at the end of Chapter 38 for the blow about to befall Pip, though the parallel to the Sultan's cutting of the fatal rope is not clear.

One final note. The trial scene in Chapter 56 (five paragraphs) shows Dickens at his best: the scene is concisely but colourfully portrayed, vivid in its contrasts; with implied condemnation of an inhuman system and shrewd glances at human failings, dignity and depravity. And there is detailed realism; and symbolism, as in the sunbeam linking Life and Eternity.

Characters

With each new novel Dickens added a set of characters to his gallery of studies of men and women unexcelled for their vitality and variety. Often their very abundance was out of all proportion to the story, but by the time he came to write *Great Expectations* he had managed to strike a closer balance between plot and characters. There is, too, a clearly drawn contrast between the simple, honest, patient and faithful folk on the one hand and the proud, avaricious, spiteful and hypocritical on the other.

Dickens had a unique gift for portraying two types: the outcast and the eccentric; here represented by Magwitch and Miss Havisham. These two, actuated by very different kinds of revenge, create between them all the complications necessary for a highly involved, though well-knit plot; a third character, the hidden villain, Compeyson, is the prime mover, since prior to the events of the story, his wickedness drove the other two to make their respective plans. Compeyson is also the ultimate instrument of fate in compassing the arrest of Magwitch, and indirectly the disappearance of Pip's fortune.

The formidable lawyer, Jaggers, and his efficient clerk, Wemmick, are 'agents', carrying out the wishes of others with the utmost discretion and a complete lack of feeling (except in Walworth); Orlick, that creeping spirit of the marshes, is the agent of everything evil; the self-effacing Joe and the shrewd, placid Biddy represent the good influences of a happy and contented, if humble home life; Herbert is a true friend to Pip, sharing his plans, rescuing him in the nick of time and enabling him in the end to make good; his successful partnership and the bequest to his father are both conferred by Miss Havisham through the influence of Pip, whose own expectations ultimately come to nothing. As Estella points out, she and Pip are really puppets, yet each makes a vital decision against his or her own interests: he deliberately refuses to accept his fortune when he knows from whom it comes; she deliberately marries a brute to spare Pip a loveless marriage.

The remaining characters are of minor importance, yet the least significant among them does not escape without some distinguishing mark by which to be remembered. Dickens believed passionately in the men and women he created, and a wide range of experience in reporting as well as his concentrated and accurate gift of observation furnished him with ample materials. Scattered through the book are vignettes from the life, of tavern landlords, lodging-house landladies, waiters, coachmen, warders, shopkeepers and boy assistants.

With all his characters, great and small, Dickens had a trick of fixing them by stressing one particular feature or gesture or by the use of a special phrase: Matthew Pocket distractedly trying to lift himself by his hair, Mr Jaggers pausing at the crucial moment with his handkerchief on the way to his nose, Mr Wemmick's 'post-office of a mouth', Joe's anticipation of happy cooperation, 'What larks!' It is this device that has given rise to the criticism that Dickens saw his characters almost entirely from without, that there is little study of inner motives and emotions.

There is certainly a wealth of gesture in this book, the hands alone being given considerable significance: Jaggers biting his forefinger when he is about to squeeze admissions out of others; Magwitch holding out both hands in order to admire the gentleman he has created; Pumblechook obsequiously shaking hands; Wemmick's hand stealing round Miss Skiffin's waist; the knitting action of the fingers peculiar to both Estella and her mother Molly, the housekeeper.

It should be noted how nearly all the characters in the book undergo a change, striking or subtle. Apart from the softened mood of Magwitch and the hysterical remorse of Miss Havisham, even the imperturbable Jaggers is betrayed into a weak moment; the otherwise steady Joe oscillates between affection for Pip and respect for 'Mr Pip'; Wemmick leads a Jekyll and Hyde existence between Walworth and Little Britain; Estella develops a tenderness towards Pip as Pip does towards Magwitch. Two vicious people show no human feeling whatever, the brute Drummle and the toady, Sarah Pocket. Otherwise there is much true sympathy expressed throughout the book by a number of those who make the briefest of appearances, such as the governor of the prison and the landlady at Chinks's Basin.

Dickens's novels are remarkable for their detailed and realistic pictures of the interiors of houses, and these usually have a close connection with the characters of their occupants. Besides Satis House, with its shutters, sheets and cobwebs, there is the carefully preserved parlour at the forge – used only once a year at Christmas while the rest of the house is undergoing a fierce cleaning-up at the hands of that merciless housekeeper, Mrs Joe; Pumblechook's premises, with their flavour of seeds tied up in brown paper packets in rows of little drawers. Then there is the Pocket household where the master and mistress are so preoccupied that their domestic affairs and large family are left in the charge of a large staff of servants; the 'Castle', where Wemmick brushes away the Newgate cobwebs by indulging his taste for engineering, carpentry, plumbing and gardening; Jaggers's room with its solid furniture, library of law books and papers brought home from the office; the office itself, small and dismal, and dominated by the two plaster-casts of executed criminals.

Food is also given considerable significance in association with character: the 'freemasonry of Pip and Joe' over their progress in nibbling the thick slices of bread doled out to them by Mrs Gargery; the gormandizing Pumblechook keeping Pip from eating by setting him sums in mental arithmetic; the Aged Parent entrusted with preparing a 'haystack' of buttered toast; Jaggers methodically dispensing wine and sauces from his dumbwaiter; Pip entertaining Herbert with a sumptuous banquet out of his own resources, and later regaling Estella on her arrival in London with a tea as bafflingly unsatisfactory as his own relationship with her; the heavy 'grubbing' of Magwitch, and Barley's huge breakfast; Miss Havisham roaming about at midnight in search of scraps. Unlike so many novelists whose characters never have time to eat, Dickens supplies some of his with complete menus!

Dickens nearly always draws attention to the eyes: Pumblechook's dull and staring; Miss Havisham's dark and flashing; Jaggers's sharp and suspicious; Wemmick's small and glittering; Biddy's thoughtful and attentive; Joe's of an undecided blue; Compeyson's shifty; Orlick's fixed on the ground; and the eye of the stranger in Chapter 10 half-shut.

Pip

The roof of my stronghold dropped upon me

Pip's self-portrait is a frank one. His recollection of the events that changed him from a humble blacksmith's boy to a young man of fashion is interspersed with reflections on his various motives, in which he does not attempt to disguise his shrinking from secret terrors, his morbid fears and his mean pretences. On the other hand, even a snob is not devoid of good intentions, and Pip, while concerned to show himself the victim of circumstances, can point to the good that he has done to others. He is, indeed, with the exception of his sister and Orlick, obviously liked by the chief characters in the book. The only two objective descriptions of him come very close together (Chapter 30): one by Herbert, and rather in his favour, 'a good fellow, with impetuosity and hesitation, boldness and diffidence, action and dreaming, curiously mixed in him'; the other, a burlesque by Trabb's Boy, who mimics his bearing and exclaims, 'Pon my soul, don't know yah!' He rejects both representations!

Pip's early experience of home life is very unhappy, and only the realization that it is 'sanctified' by Joe causes him regret at leaving it. The only survivor of six infant boys, he is made by his sister to feel that his birth is a misfortune and that he would be better in his grave. Regarded by all but Joe with abhorrence as naturally 'vicious', he is given the smallest portions of food, and, worst humiliation of all, is constantly reminded by Pumblechook, 'uncle' only in name, to be grateful to 'them which brought you up by hand'. The boy has no childhood playmate, and his sister's unmerciful use of 'Tickler' renders him deeply sensitive, obstinate and reticent. Pip suffers agonies of suspense, tells amazing lies and his imagination conjures up fearful ideas of what might happen to him. Early conflict with injustice, such as the confiscation of his small earnings, renders him morally timid.

Though used to country exercises, Pip has a habit of falling asleep and even of swooning, as when Magwitch reveals himself. He endures nightmares of apprehension, and lies awake at night or rises to listen at the window. He lives in constant dread of some discovery – the theft of the pie; his 'murder' of Uncle Pumblechook; his assault on Herbert. At such times everything wears an accusing air – the hare in the pantry or the cattle on the marshes. When faced by death in the hut by the lime-kiln, a series of visions pass rapidly through Pip's mind: everybody misconstruing his actions; his sister's illness; the murderer slouching into the village inn while his victim dissolves in vapour; his rooms at Barnard's Inn on that fatal night; the fugitive waiting in vain at Chinks's Basin. During his fever his imagination runs riot.

This is the sensitive nature that is first made conscious of being a 'common labouring boy' by the pretty girl commenting on his coarse hands and thick boots. To her teasing he owes his 'hankerings after money and gentility'. On her account particularly he shrinks from the taint of prison and crime that seems to cling to him, so that he trembles at the word 'convict' – and, ironically, it is on account of a convict's daughter! When the money is mysteriously provided, seemingly for the express purpose of his acquiring the gentility necessary to find favour in Estella's eyes, his home surroundings seem 'monotonous acquaintances' compared with the life awaiting him in London. Though Pip sheds tears at the signpost, he has avoided bringing Joe with him as far as the coach. This is the beginning of a series of subterfuges, each of which leads to a feeling of shame: when he avoids Pumblechook, he runs into Trabb's Boy; when he avoids the Blue Boar on his way to meet Orlick in the marshes and stays at a smaller inn, he has to listen to the tale of his 'ingratitude' to Pumblechook – a terrible indirect rebuke for his treatment of Joe.

Pip's inheritance quickly impresses him with the power of money. The realization of his 'wild fancy' leads him to take whatever is given him (and Magwitch's provision is that he should be educated, not for a profession, but for a life of leisure) in the belief that fate destined him to be the wealthy husband of a beautiful woman. He witnesses the toadying of Miss Havisham's relatives and the toadying, to himself, of the shopkeepers. The prospect of an unlimited purse leads him into improvidence and, in the person of the Avenger, ostentation.

For Pip's mistaken belief that Miss Havisham is his benefactress, it must be said that there were significant indications in that direction. When Jaggers informs him that the name was a profound secret, he adds, 'If you have a suspicion in your own breast, keep that suspicion in your own breast'; when Pip visits Miss Havisham before his departure for London, she recalls Sarah Pocket to gloat over the discomfiture caused by Pip's 'gay figure'. He therefore tends to forget that, after rewarding him for his wheeling of her chair with twenty-five guineas towards his apprenticeship, she has said there would be nothing more. Not until much later is he to realize that it is only by a coincidence that Miss Havisham and Magwitch employed the same lawyer; but on that coincidence is built the whole fabric of his dreams.

Pip regards money merely as a means to an end. When Estella is betrothed to Drummle he has no further use for it. In his own words, nature and circumstances have made him romantic. He worships Estella from the first meeting and continues to do so 'against all reason'. Outside the gloomy walls of Satis, Estella and her guardian are associated by him with all that is picturesque and enchanting. Not even Estella's words of warning could change a passionate devotion that, all along, is obvious to Herbert. When he discovers her parentage, some of his romantic regard for her is transferred to Magwitch. On his return to England a sentimental desire to visit the garden in which he once walked with Estella brings him face to face with her, an ending which, highly artificial as it may seem, undoubtedly satisfies our sense of what is fair. His attachment to his bedroom and the village signpost is still strong when he takes leave of Joe and Biddy before going abroad.

If Pip has much for which to be forgiven by these two, he has also much to forgive in the wrong done him by Miss Havisham and, under her influence, by Estella. That he forgives both freely (even as he can remember his sister without rancour) is proof that, beneath the surface, his true nature was not spoilt by his 'Great Expectations'.

Joe Gargery

'God bless you, dear old Pip, old chap!'

This village blacksmith stands for all that is honest, respectable, proud and affectionate among the humble poor whom Dickens knew so well. He is one of nature's gentlemen, and his character sweetens the whole book, 'a mild, good-natured, sweet-tempered, easy-going, foolish, dear fellow – a sort of Hercules in strength, and also in weakness'.

Joe is never at home outside his forge. His best clothes make him resemble a respectable scarecrow, and his manners in strange company are extraordinarily uncouth. He is amused at first by Pip's efforts to improve him, because his simple pride in his own work rejects any thought of leaving it for any 'higher sphere'. Joe stays in London only long enough to deliver his message from Miss Havisham (a message that makes Pip ashamed of his cold welcome of the messenger), and once Pip has recovered from his fever, tactfully departs for home after paying Pip's debts. The same delicate tact leads him to change the subject when Pip tries to discuss his financial predicament.

Joe sees good in everybody, even his brute of a father, and his memory of his mother makes him chivalrous to all women, even his termagant wife. He hates lies (but he deviates into fiction in order to gratify Mrs Joe with an imaginary communication of Miss Havisham's compliments). He can knock down the hulking Orlick and nurse Pip with a woman's tenderness. He warns Pip, as a 'true friend', that he would never 'get to be oncommon' through crooked ways. Throughout his interview with Miss Havisham he persists in addressing his replies to Pip in a manner 'expressive of forcible argumentation, strict confidence, and great politeness', but, when badgered by Jaggers about accepting a sum of money in compensation for losing the boy's services, he adopts a pugilistic attitude which scares the lawyer, so dreaded in town, out of the room.

Joe's speech is illiterate almost to absurdity, but conviction shines through it. Nothing is more forceful than a sentence begun by him with 'Which!' He admits he is 'awful dull' and regards the writing of a letter as the height of scholarship; yet, slowly raking the fire in the kitchen or smoking his pipe at the Three Jolly Bargemen, he 'beat out' for himself a philosophy and a code of conduct: 'Pip, dear old chap, life is made of ever so many partings *welded* together, as I may say.' His maxims, indeed, are of the simplest: 'manners is manners', when Pip had apparently bolted his slice of bread; 'lies is lies', when he finds Pip's glorified version of events at Satis is completely untrue; 'a gridiron *is* a gridiron', when Pip hankers after visiting Miss Havisham to thank her. To Joe, a blacksmith was a blacksmith, and at a loss away from his forge.

Mrs Gargery

'Drat that boy'

The blacksmith's wife – 'Mrs Joe' to her small brother – is one of those formidable women so frequently created by Dickens. Tall and bony, and given to scrubbing everybody and everything, herself included, she regards her apron as a symbol of slavery. She has a habit of forcing herself into a passion and, when Pip is to blame, punishes her husband as well. She is an unscrupulous spy and a toady to Uncle Pumblechook. On her husband, who admires in her a 'master-mind' and a 'fine figure of a woman', she lavishes the most abusive epithets, such as 'stuck pig' and 'king of the noodles'. At times she throws things at him, Pip included. Her dustpan is the sign of her wrath, just as 'Tickler' is her instrument of punishment.

Biddy

'The best wife in the whole world'

After Mrs Joe has been disabled by a more powerful blow than any she has herself inflicted, Biddy brings to Joe and his forge a complete transformation – from constant quarrels and backbiting to steady trust and affection. Plain and unassuming in manner, Biddy has more than her share of feminine intuition. Her shrewd thrusts ruffle Pip's new-found conceit of himself more than anything else, more even than Estella's taunts. She is to become the mother of a younger Pip sitting on his stool in his old corner.

Abel Magwitch

'Yes, Pip, dear boy, I've made a gentleman on you'

It is the fate of Abel Magwitch, alias Provis, alias Mr Campbell, to be twice hunted down as a fugitive from the law into whose clutches he first fell early in life through bad company. As a boy he is known as a hardened character who spends more time in gaol than out of it. As the accomplice of Compeyson (the gentleman turned crook), he is arrested and sentenced to fourteen years in the Hulks. Compeyson escapes with a seven year sentence by getting his counsel to put most of the blame on Magwitch who determines to avenge himself. Escaping from the Hulks, he brings about his own recapture by going after Compeyson who has escaped about the same time, to drag him back to prison. Magwitch's attempted escape results in transportation to Australia, and there in a lonely shepherd's hut he thinks much of the boy who had brought him food and a file without betraying him, and determines, when he inherits some property and has prospered in sheep-breeding, to turn this boy into a better gentleman than Compeyson.

If Pip has reason to feel ashamed of Joe's behaviour, he has far more reason to be disgusted by Magwitch's manners. Accustomed only to prison life or the solitudes of Australia, Magwitch, a powerful man with long iron-grey hair, eats ravenously, using his jack-knife, smokes 'negro-head' tobacco, drinks rum and water and plays Patience with a battered pack of cards. He has a peculiar click in his throat and carries a black Testament on which he not only swears oaths, but keeps himself up to his own resolutions. Magwitch's one great resolve redeems his character. In the pride of his creation he finds himself, but his determination to see in the flesh the 'gentleman what I made' leads to his second and final recapture. Towards the end he becomes strangely softened in manner and reconciled to his lot. In the bold bid for freedom Magwitch is the least anxious of the party. The old vengeful spirit flashes out when he seizes Compeyson and drags him under (a fitting end to such a villain). However, Magwitch stands trial with dignity and dies content in the knowledge that his 'gentleman' loves his own long-lost daughter.

Estella

'Pip, will you never take warning?'

The character of Magwitch's daughter, Miss Havisham's protégée and Pip's beloved, is not easy to delineate. She is the beautiful offspring of a criminal and a gypsy. Transferred to a rich but eccentric household at the age of three, Estella becomes Miss Havisham's creation in a far more complete sense than that in which Pip was Magwitch's. She submits to her training as a breaker of men's hearts, but when, beautiful and accomplished, she is reproached by Miss Havisham for denying her the affection this morbid woman has endeavoured to breed out of her, she calmly rebukes her 'mother by adoption' for such an unreasonable attitude.

Estella openly regards herself and Pip as puppets and behaves as though they are intended for each other, but candidly warns him that her heart is devoid of 'sympathy – sentiment – nonsense'. In her flowing hair and the action of her fingers when knitting she resembles her mother – whether she ever learns who her parents are we are not told. We know only that Jaggers is against her receiving the information.

Pip cannot believe that there can be such beauty without a heart. It enchants him from the day when he first hears her clear voice call from the window and sees her candle coming along the passage like a star, to the day of his passionate declaration of love, the last time he is to see her for eleven years. And on reflection, the reader may be justified in wondering whether Estella's 'inaccessibility' is not, after all, a pose. Estella has been allowed by Miss Havisham to go out into the 'daylight' to add elegance and refinement to her beauty, and thus might possibly have learned to see human relationships in truer proportion. We know that she has been warned that love is a snare, and Pip is told quite plainly that she understands such a sentiment as a mere 'form of words'; the last look she gives him is one of 'incredulous wonder' when he reveals how much she has become a part of him. Yet something of the 'bent and broken' Estella who sheds silent tears in the moonlight may be glimpsed when she not only warns Pip of his intended fate at her hands, but by her own act chooses to accept Drummle in order to spare the man 'who would soonest feel that I took nothing to him'. Twice Estella makes it clear to him that she differentiates between him and – all others. Her self-sacrifice is a heavy one, for it is not Drummle but she who is to be the victim of the marriage.

Miss Havisham

'Hear me, Pip! Love her!'

The spoilt child of a wealthy brewer; an heiress infatuated with an obvious intriguer; a bride deserted on her wedding morning; a recluse existing morbidly in a darkened house where no reckoning is kept of the passage of time – such is the strange woman who, when she has the whim to see a child play, sends for a boy from the neighbourhood. When Pip sees Miss Havisham, she reminds him of a waxwork image and a disinterred skeleton he has once seen; she resembles a witch as she hobbles about leaning on her stick, with which she is accustomed to emphasize her remarks. She gloats over the discomfiture of her jealous relatives and the beauty of the girl she has adopted and named. She urges Pip to love Estella in a tone that suggests hate rather than love.

Dickens calls her mania the 'vanity of sorrow'. By living such a solitary life she shuts out all healthy influences and suffers for it, mentally and physically. Her remorse begins when Pip unfolds his love for Estella; she holds her hand to her heart and her face assumes a ghastly look. Her death is caused by brooding over the fire until her faded bridal dress, tattered and highly inflammable, catches fire. Though she seeks to quench love in Estella, Miss Havisham yearns for it for herself and calls the girl ungrateful; in the terrible scene in which she reproaches herself – 'What have I done?' – she explains that at first she intended only to save Estella from a misery like her own. In Pip's ardent young face she sees the love she herself has once felt; in trying to save her life he suffers burns that are nothing compared with the emotional torment she has caused him.

Mr Jaggers

'I didn't say so, Mr Pip. I am putting a case'

True to his description of himself as a mere 'agent', Mr Jaggers originates nothing, evil or good, but carries out the commission of others. Before the events which happen in the book he does, indeed, choose Estella for Miss Havisham's adopted daughter (just as Pumblechook chose Pip when asked for a playmate for Estella), but thereafter he does what he is paid to do and no more.

Nevertheless, Jaggers's dominating personality gives him an aspect of fate itself. To him the human race is always in trouble, children being 'spawned' to find their way, sooner or later, into the 'net' of himself and others of his profession. He impresses all whom he meets with the idea that he knows something about them 'to their disadvantage'. Herbert is probably not the only one to come away from a conversation with him feeling that he has committed some crime. His formidable manner terrifies all with whom he comes into contact or who know him only by reputation – clerks, turnkeys, coachmen, even the judge on his bench – and he positively defies burglars to enter his premises. Jaggers bullies everybody and everything, from witnesses in court to the very sandwich he is munching. His cross-examination extends to a chance acquaintance in an inn, like the unfortunate Wopsle, and even to the wine he drinks.

In his practice Jaggers adheres always to 'the strict line of fact'; he demands exact figures and forces those with whom he has to deal to make definite statements. He makes no admissions and, in fairness, warns others not to commit themselves. 'Take nothing on its looks; take everything on evidence', is his motto. He makes no recommendations and allows no questions (this is Wemmick's province). Until absolute proof is forthcoming or where the slightest caution is necessary, Jaggers prefers to treat the subject under discussion as purely hypothetical. He draws a significant distinction between Pip's being 'told' by Magwitch and his being 'informed'.

Pip never forgets the details of Jaggers's appearance at their first chance meeting on the stairs at Satis, and he checks them off when he encounters him again at the village inn:

> His large head, his dark complexion, his deep-set eyes, his bushy black eyebrows, his large watch-chain, his strong black dots of beard and whisker, and even the smell of scented soap on his great hand.

Jaggers regularly washes his hands and face after hours as if washing off his clients; and the halo of scented soap precedes him as he forces his way through the unfortunates hanging about his office door. The wall opposite his chair is greasemarked by the shoulders of those who endure his relentless questionings. The brass nails on his high-backed chair remind Pip of a coffin, as the loops of the carved garlands on the panelled walls of the lawyer's rooms remind him of the hangman's noose.

Jaggers never laughs and never relaxes, except once when he actually sighs when Wemmick ventures to suggest that he might be looking forward to a pleasant home in his retirement. Only once does he give a slight sign of being startled – when Pip tells him who Estella's father was. The inflexible manner, however, swiftly returns, a manner which, Wemmick explains, is purely professional and intended to puzzle. While awaiting an answer, Jaggers sways forward till his boots creak, or pauses with an enormous silk handkerchief – his chief weapon – in his hands halfway to his nose. This very gesture is often sufficient in itself to elicit the information he wants. When he grows impatient or utters a warning he frowns and bites his huge forefinger at his victim.

It is Jaggers's phrase that gives the book its title. He sees Pip making a wrong assumption and could put him right with a hint, but this would mean violating his professional code of honour. He is not the least remarkable of Dickens's set of men of law.

Wemmick

'Official sentiments are one thing. We are extra-official'

Unlike his chief, Wemmick leaves the office behind him when he goes home to the suburb of Walworth. Here he indulges his fancy as a 'Jack-of-all-trades' with a variety of devices too numerous for a small wooden cottage and garden, were it not that everything is on a miniature scale. In the genial atmosphere of the 'Walworth sentiment' Pip feels at home as nowhere else since his departure from the forge; he certainly is given kindly advice which would never have been proffered in the office where business is conducted in a formal and even hostile spirit. Wemmick is seen at his best in his tender treatment of the Aged Parent, who is regularly nodded at, patiently listened to while he reads from the newspaper, and allowed to fire the gun and work the drawbridge.

No one has surpassed Dickens in the presentation of genuine home life, and the simplicity, regularity and wholesomeness of the 'Castle' is in strong contrast to the fantastic state of affairs at Hammersmith.

Wemmick's most pronounced feature is his 'post-office slit' of a mouth, set in a square, wooden face. His respect for his employer is considerable; he carries official precaution to an extreme, as when he requests the immediate burning of the letter warning Pip to get Magwitch away, an obscurely worded missive that could have given nobody away.

Even when Wemmick arranges his wedding, his secretive methods have the upper hand, and an innocent fishing expedition is turned, by a series of surprises, into a perfectly organized ceremony at a quiet country church. A last touch is his depositing of his white gloves in the font on leaving. Miss Skiffins, equally wooden in appearance, equally methodical in her ways, and long accustomed to the routine at the 'Castle', though now a 'Walworth sentiment' on no account to be mentioned to Mr Jaggers, would undoubtedly, besides managing his fowls, effect such a change in Wemmick from his customary bachelor appearance as would hardly escape that vigilant eye. Then, it may be supposed, they would be on bad terms with one another, until some unfortunate client offered himself for browbeating and enabled them to re-establish a good understanding on the old footing of professional inflexibility!

While Mr Jaggers maintained a judicial ignorance of the ex-convict's whereabouts, Wemmick spares no pains to keep a close watch on developments. His motto is, 'Get hold of portable property', and his person is decked with mementoes of executed clients.

Herbert

My intimate companion and friend

If Pip is deprived of childhood companionship, he is blessed as a young man with a sympathetic and true friend. Herbert has been 'tried' by Miss Havisham, presumably for Estella to practise upon, but has failed, as he was likely to fail in his realization of 'Capital', had not Pip created a partnership for him. When first encountered pale, pimply and angular, and determind on sparring with Pip in the garden at Satis, Herbert takes the blows dealt him by Pip with the same airy inconsequence with which he later withstands the 'buffets of poverty' while 'looking about him' in London. Herbert's only qualification for success in life is a hopeful disposition. He is, however, a frank and easy companion and gives Pip sound advice, and, though he expresses admiration of the latter's businesslike way of ticking off their debts and allowing a 'margin', Pip has to admit that, given his 'opening', Herbert is to prove the better businessman. He is fortunate, too, in the devotion of Clara Barley, a 'captive fairy' attendant on her 'ogre' of a father. When these two are married out in the East, 'Handel' is to find a third home with them.

Minor characters

The background of the story is well filled with lesser characters encountered by Pip. Some of these are given whole episodes to themselves, with little bearing on the plot, but providing interest as sketches, or in some cases caricatures from real life; others appear once only and are not heard of again. However, with few exceptions, and no matter how odd their idiosyncracies, they convey the impression of being very much alive, an achievement in characterization which is Dickens's supreme gift as a novelist. For convenience they are here sketched in groups.

Pumblechook that 'liar and hypocrite' is foremost among the visitors at the forge. He has 'a mouth like a fish, dull staring eyes, and sandy hair standing upright on his head'. Little in fiction is more despicable than his claim to be Pip's benefactor: after heaping insults and arithmetical sums on the blacksmith's boy, Pumblechook goes out of his way to shake hands with the young man of fortune and even tries to wheedle him into investing money into his business. When Pumblechook is ignored, he fills the press and the neighbourhood with his lies; when Pip, his prospects ruined and his health impaired, stops at the Blue Boar on his way back to Joe, the old impostor delivers a pompous lecture to him on this ingratitude.

Mr Wopsle, the parish clerk, with his Roman nose and deep, declamatory voice reappears in London as a Shakesperian actor. Having failed in this role we later see him in an amazing variety of stage parts. 'Mr Waldengarver' as Hamlet and later in pantomine is given the best part of two chapters (31 and 47) for his extraordinary performances, together with the reactions of his audience, not to mention his recitation of George Barnwell and his dramatic reading of the murder case in which he is so sharply pulled up by Mr Jaggers. His great-aunt's academy is the most farcical burlesque in the book.

Orlick is more sinister than Compeyson simply because we see more of his slouching figure, 'dancing' at Biddy, creeping up behind Mrs Joe to fell her with the cast-off leg-iron, or drunkenly preparing to kill Pip and burn his body in the lime kiln. He ends up in gaol for the burglary of Pumblechook's shop. Nothing Orlick does, not even his spying or his melodramatic attempt on Pip's life, has any influence on the plot (Mrs Joe might have been made to die a natural death); the chief reason for his existence would seem to be to make the reader's flesh creep.

Sarah Pocket is equally sinister but quite harmless: in her wig and hideous muslin cap she keeps the door at Satis, growing ever more green and yellow at the thought of others benefiting from Miss Havisham's will, and receiving in the end only twenty-five pounds a year for her services. The other toadies, Georgiana and Camilla, are similarly served.

In London, we are taken to the Hammersmith household once and no more.

Matthew Pocket, who so offended Miss Havisham by telling her the truth about Compeyson, manages, by tutoring young gentlemen and doing some literary hack-work, to maintain a large family in a respectable riverside residence, staffed by a retinue of servants. Distracted by frequent domestic mishaps, he gives ludicrous expression to his helplessness and perplexity by trying to lift himself up by his hair, and our last glimpse of him is in a state of collapse on the sofa after a particularly inane remark by his wife.

Mrs Pocket is one more example of the author's unsympathetic treatment of the upper-classes or those who lay claim to gentility of birth or breeding: Drummle is a boor, Compeyson a villain, Miss Havisham unbalanced, the Finches empty-headed and the Brandleys mere ciphers in the story. Daughter of a would-be baronet and mother of seven children 'tumbling up', Mrs Pocket spends hours poring over family pedigrees, oblivious of the things she leaves lying about. Her 'aristocratic disposition' being so accustomed to luxury and elegance, she might be ornamental, but, as mistress of a household, completely useless. Like Miss Havisham she has an attendant toady in Mrs Coiler.

Bentley Drummle, the 'Spider' as Jaggers nicknames him, is really a well-bred Orlick, being two removes from a baronetcy; 'idle, proud, niggardly, reserved and suspicious', he is content to lie in wait for his opportunity. Drummle sneers at others for lending him money and toasts Estella with a leer at Pip. The ensuing challenge comes to nothing, as Estella accepts his addresses and finally marries him, enduring many years of ill-treatment at his hands.

Startop, though spoilt as a boy, is an agreeable, forgiving young man, who assists Pip and Herbert on the day of the attempted escape abroad.

Clara Barley, a rather demure young lady, disliked her lover's 'expensive companion' on principle and Pip does not get to meet Herbert's betrothed for some time. He finds her to be gentle and confiding, but subject to her tyrant father, a former ship's purser who, when not stamping on the floor for attention, or doling out his 'sotres', or sweeping the river with his telescope, lies on the bed muttering a blasphemous refrain about himself.

Chapter summaries, textual notes and revision questions

First stage

Chapter 1

One bleak Christmas Eve in the marshlands of North Kent, a young boy stands looking at the graves of his parents and five younger brothers. Pip (Philip Pirrip) has been brought up by his sister who is married to the local blacksmith Joe Gargery. Frightened and lonely Pip begins to cry when a fearful man covered in mud and with an iron on his leg appears before him. The man questions Pip about his family and tells him to bring a file and some 'wittles' to the Old Battery the following morning.

marsh country The marshy North Kent peninsula lying between the estuaries of the Thames and the Medway.
wittles Slang for victuals i.e. food.

Chapter 2

Pip runs home from the churchyard only to learn from his hen-pecked brother-in-law that his wife has been out looking for him a dozen times and is now out on a renewed search with 'Tickler' (a wax-ended piece of cane). Pip is doubly miserable as not only does he suffer his sister's tongue on her return, but he must also forfeit his tea if he is to keep his promise to the convict. He is given a dose of tar-water for bolting his bread which he has in fact concealed in his trouser leg for the morrow.

On hearing guns firing, Pip learns that this is done to alert the locality that a prisoner has escaped from the Hulks (prison ships). True to his promise, early next morning Pip sets off for the marshes with food and brandy for his strange friend.

Hercules The personification of superhuman physical strength in Greek mythology.
jack-towel Roller-towel (see the first paragraph of Chapter 26).
plaister Poultice.
larcenous researches Searches for something to steal.

Tar-water An infusion of tar in cold water, once used as a medicine.
boot-jack An instrument for pulling off boots.

Chapter 3

On his way to the Battery, Pip comes across a man sitting with his back to him, nodding with sleep; presuming him to be 'his' convict, Pip creeps up and gently touches him on the shoulder. To his horror, he discovers that this is a different convict, who swiftly aims a blow at Pip and disappears into the mist. When Pip tells 'his' convict of this strange meeting, his man becomes excited and quickly files at his leg iron. Indeed he is so engrossed in his filing that he doesn't notice Pip slipping away.

Chapter 4

Christmas dinner is passed in a state of suspense by Pip, squeezed into a corner, fed on scraps and generally abused. When Mr Pumblechook comments on the richness of the pork and Mrs Joe offers him some brandy, Pip knows that all is lost: he has substituted tar-water for brandy. Mr Pumblechook drinks it down in one go with amazing results: he begins leaping around and making horrible grimaces much to the consternation of the gathered company. He demands some hot gin and water and fortunately Mrs Joe is too busy preparing this concoction to wonder how the tar-water came to be in the brandy bottle.

Pip has only just begun to relax when Mrs Joe orders her husband to bring on clean plates for the pork pie (which Pip has also given to the convict). As his sister heads for the pantry, a terrified Pip rushes from the table, out of the house and headlong into a party of soldiers who have brought some handcuffs to be repaired.

Sunday penitentials i.e. best clothes.
Accoucheur Policeman i.e. he had been 'arrested' at birth. (*Accoucheur* is French for a male midwife. The word is also used by fashionable women to describe the doctor who delivers their baby.)
Roman nose A nose with a prominent upper part or bridge, like those seen in portraits of ancient Romans.
religious cross ... Richard the Third i.e. sepulchral and yet declamatory tones. Hamlet and Richard the Third are two well-known characters in Shakespeare, in the plays to which they give their name.

restless people i.e. they conquered an empire.
a Medium In Spiritualism a person communicating with the unseen, at whose seances furniture is said to move of itself.

Chapter 5

Joe repairs the handcuffs; and he, Pip and Mr Wopsle join the soldiers as they set off across the marshes in search of the two escaped convicts. They find them fighting in a ditch and once they are separated, Pip's convict confesses, of his own volition, to stealing food and drink from the blacksmith's house. Both convicts are led away to the prison ships.

stocks Pieces of wood into which the barrel of a firearm was fixed.
She drew a pitcher of beer ... brandy Notice the distinction in drinks according to rank, which would find little favour today.
Hob and nob A familiar invitation to have a drink.
Musical Glasses A collection of glasses holding graduated amounts of water and 'played' by striking them or by rubbing a moistened finger around their rims.
sauce for dinner i.e. their appetite was increased by the excitement.
Tar See note on 'Tar-water'. p.47.

Chapter 6

Pip feels that he should confess his crimes to Joe but he is afraid of losing Joe's love and opts instead to keep them secret. Meanwhile Mr Pumblechook and Mr Wopsle are busy theorizing as to how the convict got into the house to steal the goods.

untaught genius i.e. he had learned by himself to behave like a moral coward.

Chapter 7

A year later, Pip who by his own efforts and some help from Biddy has learned elementary reading, writing and arithmetic writes a letter to Joe on his slate. He now learns that Joe has enjoyed even less education than he has. Their talk is interrupted by Mrs Joe and Mr Pumblechook, who arrive with the news that Pip is to be sent to Miss

Havisham who seeks a boy to 'play' at her home. Pip is to spend the night at the Pumblechooks before being delivered to Miss Havisham the following morning.

Mark Antony's oration In Shakespeare's *Julius Caesar*, III,2.
Collins's *Ode on the Passions* The relevant passage is:

Revenge impatient rose:
He threw his blood-stain'd sword in thunder down;
And with a withering look
The war-denouncing trumpet took.

elaborated i.e. dressed for the occasion.
comes the Mo-gul Tyrannizes. The Moguls were absolute rulers of India from 1526 to 1707.
on the Ram-page A slang expression for 'behaving violently'.
Pompeyed Pampered.

Chapter 8

Pip is summarily delivered to Satis House the next day. He is met at the door by a beautiful young girl who, although no older than he, is both self-possessed and scornful of him. He is taken to meet Miss Havisham who commands him to play cards with Estella. The young girl comments on the coarseness of his hands and general appearance, causing Pip to feel shame at his background. Miss Havisham tells him to return in six days and orders that before he leaves he be given some food. However, this is done so ungraciously by Estella that Pip suffers great humiliation at his treatment and is reduced to tears.

The cold wind ... there Notice the sympathetic background.
my sister's working me Cf. the threat in the previous chapter.
I looked about me ... hide my face in Dickens had often been in this position.

Chapter 9

As soon as Pip comes home, Mrs Joe cross-examines him about his visit to Satis and when Mr Pumblechook arrives at the house, he too joins in the cross-examination. Pip invents fantastic stories to satisfy their curiosity but later feeling remorse, confesses to Joe that the stories were nothing but lies. Joe is shocked by Pip's dishonesty and warns him against lying again. He also tells him that he must overcome his feelings of inferiority.

caparisoned coursers Horses with covering cloths.

Chapter 10

Pip decides that the best way to rid himself of his commonness would be with the help of Biddy, who on this particular evening is teaching him all she can from her Catalogue of Prices. When the lessons are over, Pip calls for Joe at the Three Jolly Bargemen. He finds Joe and Mr Wopsle drinking in the company of a stranger, who stirs his rum and water with the file given by Pip to the convict. As Pip and Joe leave, the stranger hands Pip a shilling wrapped in some paper which he later discovers to be a couple of pound notes.

luminous conception Bright idea.
chump-end Thick end.
dip-candle and no snuffers A dip-candle was a homemade candle, made by dipping a wick over and over again in tallow. Each time a surface of tallow adhered and eventually the candle was thick enough for use. The wicks of old-fashioned candles did not automatically burn down, but hung over and burnt all the candle away in a high flame, unless they were 'snuffed'. Snuffers were the special kind of scissors for this purpose, with a small box attached to catch the 'snuff'.
he showed no hair Convicts had their hair cut very short, so he had not long been out of prison.
old discomfiture i.e. his soaked trousers.
snarling passage from Richard the Third There is much invective in this play.
ophthalmic Of the eye, in this case pulling Pip's hair over his eyes.

Revision questions on Chapters 1–10

1 Describe and account for the companionship of Pip and Joe.

2 Give an account of Pip's experience at Satis.

3 Mention the various consequences of the convict's escape.

Chapter 11

On his next visit to Satis House, Pip meets Miss Havisham's toadying relatives. In their presence, he walks 'Miss Havisham round the decaying wedding-feast as she points to the places they are to stand when she is laid out. Once again he is compelled to play cards with Estella who treats him in her usual contemptuous manner and again once the game is over, he is left to wander in the gardens. Here he meets a young boy who insists on boxing with him; Pip is rather surprised to see his opponent go down at the first blow but admires his fighting spirit as the boy gets up and continues to fight until he finally concedes Pip's superior strength.

épergne A centre-piece for the dinner table.
seconding himself i.e. acting as a second treats a boxer.

Chapter 12

Pip's main duty at Satis House now consists in wheeling Miss Havisham every second day around the rooms of her choice. She continues to take malicious delight in his admiration of Estella. One day, however, Miss Havisham notices that Pip is growing taller; she asks him to bring Joe to her with the apprenticeship indentures.

a better speculation i.e. a black female slave might have made a kinder wife.

Chapter 13

Miss Havisham gives Joe twenty-five guineas (as a reward to Pip) for the boy's premium. Joe is completely at a loss in this strange house in the company of this even stranger woman and demonstrates his unease by addressing all his comments to Pip. They leave Satis and head for Mr Pumblechook's house where Mrs Joe is somewhat mollified by the message her husband supposedly brings from Miss Havisham. After the signing of the articles at the Town Hall, the family celebrate with a dinner, though one not at all enjoyed by the new apprentice.

court-suit A suit worn on state occasions (literally at court).
beaver i.e. of soft beaver fur.
pattens Overshoes; wooden-soled shoes with rings or bars of iron under the wood to keep them out of the mud.
Cleopatra The famous 'sovereign lady' who, when summoned to appear before Mark Antony, put on her most ravishing attire and captivated him. She has been made more famous by Shakespeare's *Antony and Cleoparta.*
on the Rampage See note p.49.
epitaph Joe composes an impromptu couplet like that 'stuck out' as an epitaph for his father (cf. Chapter 7).
hardbake Almond toffee.

Chapter 14

Once Pip had been proud to think that some day he would be apprenticed to Joe but now he feels nothing but shame – though he takes care not to reveal his real feelings to Joe. He lives in dread of finding Estella looking in at him in the forge.

Chapter 15

Pip asks Joe to be allowed to visit Miss Havisham again; though not in favour of the idea at first, Joe finally concedes to Pip's wish under the condition that the visit be regarded as experimental and, if it is not encouraged by Miss Havisham, it is never to be repeated again. However, Pip's half-day holiday causes problems as Orlick, Joe's employee, accuses his employer of favouritism. Joe seeks to keep the peace by closing the forge for the half day. Unfortunately this move does not find favour with Mrs Joe: aggravated by her comments, Orlick insults her to her face and Joe finds himself having to knock the man down for his impudence.

Pip sets off to see Miss Havisham in a troubled state of mind. Though she receives him grudgingly at first, when she realizes that there are no ulterior motives behind his visit she tells him that he may visit her now and again on his birthdays. Pip learns that Estella is now in a finishing school and again Miss Havisham torments him with memories of Estella. The visit leaves Pip feeling more discontented than ever.

On his return after a recital by Wopsle at Pumblechook's parlour, Pip finds that his sister has been struck unconscious by an unknown assailant.

expected something of her Notice how this affects the reader's idea of the significance of the title.

journeyman A qualified workman who has served his apprenticeship.

Cain or the Wandering Jew Cain was destined to be 'a fugitive and a vagabond . . . in the earth' (after he had murdered Abel, Genesis, 4,12). The legend of the Wandering Jew was that he was destined to wander about the world until Christ's second coming because he taunted Christ as he bore his cross to Calvary and urged him to go faster. The legend has been made the subject of many works.

noodles Simpletons.

dunder-headed Stupid.

George Barnwell A very popular domestic tragedy by George Lillo (1731), based on an old ballad.

Newgate A famous London prison which was demolished in 1902.

Bosworth Field The final battle in *Richard the Third*, where the king was defeated.

Glastonbury Where, according to legend, the tomb of King Arthur and Queen Guinevere was discovered. Mr Wopsle's successive fate indicates the thoughts going through the mind of Pip.

Chapter 16

The only clue to the crime is a convict's leg-iron. Orlick has a perfect alibi and the Bow Street runners are unable to trace the culprit though they suspect Joe, of all people. Mrs Joe is very ill for a long time and clearly an attendant is necessary. Biddy now takes charge of the household.

snuff See note on 'dip-candle and no snuffers', p.50.

Bow Streetmen The famous 'runners' who acted as detectives until 1829.

Chapter 17

Pip now falls into the regular routine of apprenticeship life; the only break in the routine being the annual visit to Miss Havisham on his birthday. He begins to notice Biddy more and finds her constancy contrasts sharply with Estella's capriciousness. Biddy becomes Pip's confidante and he determines to protect her from Orlick's unwanted advances.

Chapter 18

During the fourth year of his apprenticeship, Pip meets a Mr Jaggers whom he recognizes as having met once before at Miss Havisham's. Jaggers reveals that he is a lawyer from London acting on behalf of an unknown benefactor who has provided funds for Pip's education. The only conditions are that Pip never seeks to find out the name of his benefactor and that he keeps the name of Pip. Jaggers suggests that Pip move to London the following week and also recommends that Pip be placed in the care of a tutor named Matthew Pocket. The unknown benefactor has also made a sum available to buy the boy's freedom from service: Joe deeply resents this 'compensation' as he clearly regards Pip as more than an apprentice and no money can compensate for the loss of a friend.

Now that this opportunity to improve himself has come his way, Pip is uneasy about leaving Joe and Biddy.

Timon of Athens ... Coriolanus Respectively a misanthrope and a proud aristocrat who turns traitor. They are the title parts in two of Shakespeare's plays.

great expectations The student should notice on what occasions the title phrase is introduced into the story.

Chapter 19

Pip asks Biddy to help Joe towards gaining a broader view on life and when she suggests that he might be too proud to attempt to better his station in life, Pip accuses Biddy of being jealous of his new found fortune. Pip now learns the true value of money: its power. Suddenly all and sundry treat him with a respect he has never before enjoyed and even Mr Pumblechook suggests that there might be an opening in his firm for a young man of capital. Before leaving for London, Pip pays his respects to Miss Havisham who has already been informed by Jaggers of the boy's good fortune.

Pip makes his own way to the coach station but later is filled with remorse for not having allowed Joe the pleasure of seeing him off.

press Cupboard.

Mother Hubbard Who, in the nursery rhyme, went to the cupboard to find her poor dog a bone.

Barnwell parlour The place of the recital in Chapter 15.
No Thoroughfares i.e. normally not to be eaten, formerly given to Pip at home.
flip Beer and spirits mixed, sweetened and heated, a popular drink at the time.
throwing an old shoe For good luck.

Revision questions on Chapters 11–19

1 Describe the relationship at different times between Pip and Biddy.

2 In what ways does Pip show himself to be somewhat priggish after he hears of his good fortune?

3 Write short character sketches of Wopsle and Orlick.

Second stage

Chapter 20

Pip is disappointed by his first impressions of London. Mr Jaggers explains the arrangements that have been made for his accommodation: Pip is to go to Matthew Pocket's son at Barnard's Inn and stay with him until Monday when he will be taken to meet Matthew Pocket. Wemmick the clerk is to accompany him to his new lodgings.

Cross Keys Dickens first arrived here from Kent in 1822.
Little Britain A street in London.
blacks Smuts.
asmear with filth . . . foam So it remained until the Central Meat Market was built there in 1869.

Chapter 21

Barnard's Inn proves to be a dismal, dingy and shabby collection of buildings. On the top floor, a card announces that Mr Pocket Junior will be back shortly. Wemmick then departs leaving Pip to await his new companion. When he does arrive half an hour late, Pip is surprised to find that it is none other than the boy with whom he fought in the garden at Satis though now grown into a young man (Herbert Pocket).

a post-office of a mouth i.e. like the slit in a pillar-box.
pottle Small wicker basket, specially used for holding strawberries.
Covent Garden Market London's principal vegetable and fruit market at that time.

Chapter 22

Over a meal provided by Pip, Herbert tells Pip (whom he calls 'Handel') the story of Miss Havisham. On the death of her father, Miss Havisham had come into a small fortune and though her half-brother had not suffered unduly under his father's will, he bore her a grudge for her larger share. Shortly after, Miss Havisham fell passionately in love with a young man who persuaded her to buy out her brother's share in the family brewery for a vastly inflated sum. Disregarding the advice of friends and family, she did as she was bid by her fiancé. No sooner was the deed done than her fiancé called off the wedding and Miss Havisham came to understand that she had been the victim of a confidence trickster: fiancé and brother had been working together all along. Henceforth, the clocks were stopped at Satis and Miss Havisham had lived just as she was living when Pip first met her.

On the Monday morning, after accompanying Herbert to the dingy office where he is employed, Pip is taken to the Pocket home at Hammersmith where he is to live part of the time.

Barnard's Inn Associated with Gray's Inn, one of the old inns of Court, where law students congregated.
the Harmonious Blacksmith The popular name of an air with variations by Handel.
circumjacent Situated round about (cf. *ad*jacent).
fluey Covered with bits of fluff, paper etc.

Chapter 23

The Pocket household is introduced: Mr Pocket is driven frantic by his wife's incompetence, and Mrs Pocket's sole obsession is with family titles. Pip also makes the acquaintance of a widow named Coiler and two students of Mr Pocket's, Drummle and Startop.

mount to the Woolsack ... mitre i.e. become Lord Chancellor or a bishop. The Lord Chancellor sits on the 'Woolsack' in the House of Lords and a mitre signifies a bishop.
Grinder i.e. a 'crammer' of students.
refurbished ... occasions i.e. coached them for examinations.

Chapter 24

After obtaining an advance to furnish his rooms, Pip is shown Jagger's staff of clerks and taken to see the lawyer in action at court.

Australia Notice this casual reference.
the Bailey i.e. the court at the Old Bailey.
a smelter i.e. of sealing wax etc.
he was taken down i.e. his body was taken down from the gallows.
put the supposed testators to sleep i.e. murdered those in whose interests the wills were forged.
It don't signify It is of no importance.

Chapter 25

Pip's education progresses under the tuition of Mr Pocket – and his son. Wemmick entertains him at the 'Castle'.

cracksmen Burglars.
Britannia metal An alloy resembling silver.
repeater A watch that struck the hour, quarters and minute intervals at will.
bijou Ring.
roasting-jack A small revolving machine which turned round a spit on which the meat hung before the fire.

Chapter 26

Pip and his friends are entertained by Jaggers. After dinner and under the influence of wine, Drummle boasts of his prowess in rowing and to prove his point bares his muscles. Jaggers thereupon orders his housekeeper to display her powerful wrists. During a dispute about lending money, Drummle is just prevented by Jaggers from throwing a glass at Startop.

A month later Drummle leaves Mr Pocket's to the great relief of everyone but Mrs Pocket.

what kind of loops . . . like i.e. hangman's loops.
dumb-waiter Shelves revolving round a stand, for dishes etc.
Witches' caldron The apparitions in *Macbeth*, IV, 1.

Chapter 27

Joe visits Pip in London to their mutual embarrassment. Pip learns that Wopsle has left the church for the stage and that Joe has been sent by Miss Havisham to inform Pip that Estella is back home. Though now pressed to stay, Joe wishes to leave as he is aware of their changing relationship. His old friend's simple dignity moves Pip who rushes out to find him but Joe has already disappeared.

Roscian Roscius was a famous Roman actor, close to Cicero.
in the highest . . . Bard i.e. in *Hamlet*.
'Amen!' Wopsle's hecklers know his origin as parish-clerk!
wittles See note p.46.
shay-cart i.e. chaise-cart.

Chapter 28

Pip travels on the same coach as two convicts under guard, one of whom he recognizes as the one who gave him the two pound notes. He hears him talking of the incident, and knows that it was a reward for feeding the convict on the marshes and keeping his secret. At the Blue Boar (where he stays instead of at the forge, of which he feels rather ashamed) he reads an account in the local paper drawing attention to Pumblechook as his earliest benefactor.

the Tap i.e. the tap-room.
Great Remonstrance The protest against Wopsle's noisy recitation in Chapter 13. From the 'Grand Remonstrance' against Charles I measures adopted by the Long Parliament.

Telemachus Devoted son of Ulysses and Penelope.
Quintin Matsys Quentin Massys (1466–1530) was a Flemish painter who worked as a blacksmith before moving to Antwerp.
VERB SAP Short for *verbum sapienti*, a word to the wise is enough.

Chapter 29

At Satis, where Orlick is now the porter, Pip finds Estella grown into a beautiful woman. When he escorts her on a tour of the deserted grounds, she warns him that she has no tenderness of heart. Miss Havisham urges him to love her utterly. After dinner, at which they are joined by Jaggers, Pip returns to the Blue Boar, where he soon recovers from his remorse at leaving Joe unvisited.

in Paris No doubt Dickens is thinking of the Bastille.
rewarded me i.e. by a kiss.
What was it? A look of her mother, Jaggers' housekeeper?
her white hand Molly's wrists?

Chapter 30

In avoiding Pumblechook, Pip encounters Trabb's boy, who openly mocks him in the High Street. Back in London he tells Herbert of his love for Estella and is told in turn of Herbert's engagement to Clara (Barley). Herbert and Pip decide to see Wopsle in *Hamlet.*

our gift-horse's mouth Referring to the proverb, 'Never look a gift horse in the mouth' (i.e. to see how old it is – as one would do in *buying* a horse).
Denmark The setting for *Hamlet.*

Chapter 31

The play is a complete farce and Mr Wopsle bears the brunt of the audience's comments. After it has finished, Pip and Herbert go back-stage and congratulate Mr Wopsle on his performance, to his great delight. They take him home to supper and Mr Wopsle stays up until the early hours of the morning, reviewing his success.

the place of reference i.e. the cue.
that undecided Prince i.e. Hamlet.

Revision questions on Chapters 20–31

1 Describe the friendship between Pip and Herbert.

2 How many characters in these chapters turn up unexpectedly and on what occasions?

3 With how many aspects of London life does Pip become familiar?

Chapter 32

Notified by Estella of her coming to London, Pip goes very early to the coach station to meet her and, having plenty of time, in the meantime visits Newgate Prison with Wemmick.

a shoot i.e. a new arrival in prison.
his post-office See note on 'a post-office of a mouth', p.56, and early in Chapter 21.
dead plant A prisoner condemned to death.
the nameless shadow More vague suspense. Molly's hands or a premonition that Estella was connected with a convict?

Chapter 33

Pip escorts Estella to Richmond, where she is to stay with a lady willing to introduce her into society. He learns that he is expected by Miss Havisham to accompany Estella on social occasions.

pattens See note p.52.
twigs Tea-stalks.
post-coach A coach for hire (usually kept at inns).
patches Small pieces of black silk or plaster worn by ladies in the eighteenth century to show off their complexion (by contrast).

Chapter 34

Pip has allowed himself to get into debt and Herbert has followed suit. Every so often they examine their debts but nothing is ever done.
A letter brings news of the death of Pip's sister.

like Camilla See Chapter 11.
the canary-breasted Avenger See early in Chapter 27.
the apron A leather covering in an open carriage to keep off the rain.
dignities i.e. titles and titled people.
Cupid i.e. a small boy (from Cupid, the young Roman god of love).

Chapter 35

Pip returns home to attend his sister's funeral. Biddy tells him that she will be leaving the forge as she hopes to get a job teaching in the village. Pip promises to visit Joe regularly though Biddy's non-committal reply suggests that she has little faith in his words. Indeed, when Pip leaves the following morning he too harbours doubts about his promise.

others ... should be softened i.e. Estella.
a postboy i.e. a boy employed as a postilion or to look after the horses in any way.
housing A cloth covering for a horse.
doing 'Being done' was a construction only just coming into common use.

Chapter 36

On Pip's twenty-first birthday, he is told by Jaggers that he can afford to live at the rate of £500 per year, but is refused any further information about his benefactor. Pip consults Wemmick about investing some of his money for the benefit of a friend, and the latter's reply suggests that they could talk more freely at his home in Walworth.

in Little Britain i.e. Jaggers's office.
in earnest As a confirmation, a sign of the bona-fides.
his thief-dreaded watch See Chapter 25.

Chapter 37

At Walworth, Pip meets Wemmick's lady friend Miss Skiffins and Wemmick recommends that Pip employs Miss Skiffins's brother as an agent to buy a partnership. Pip emphasizes the need to keep his part in this matter secret from Herbert. A week later Pip learns from Wemmick that if he is willing to pay the sum of £250, Herbert may enter the firm of Clarriker with a view to an eventual partnership. Arrangements are made so that Herbert believes his new found fortune to be based on a chance meeting with Clarriker.

the Castle See Chapter 25.
in the post-office ... service i.e. her mouth was similar to that of Wemmick.
portable property. See towards the end of the previous chapter.
jorum A large drinking vessel.

Chapter 38

This is the one chapter entirely given to Estella: Pip describes the torture of accompanying her about London; her quarrel with Miss Havisham; Drummle's toast and his own challenge rendered void by Estella's recognition of Drummle; his reproaching her for encouraging such a fellow; and her admission that she is willing to entrap her many admirers – all of them except Pip.

Chapter 39

Pip is now twenty-three and with Herbert has moved to rooms in the Temple. On a stormy night (note the sympathetic background) Magwitch finds Pip alone and reveals himself as his unknown benefactor. Feeling more repugnance than gratitude, Pip learns that Magwitch has saved every penny to make him a 'gentleman' and that he has risked his life by returning to England from Australia in order to see the result.

the Temple The headquarters of lawyers, who have carried on their practice there for some six centuries and whose privileges have been closely guarded. Garden-court was part of the Temple precincts. Dickens was for a time a clerk in a solicitor's office and shows a good knowledge of legal practice in his novels.
warmint Bit of vermin (slang).

Revision questions on Chapters 32–39

1 Describe the relationship between Pip and Estella.

2 What part is played in these chapters by money affairs?

3 How many houses does Pip visit in this part of the story and for what reasons?

4 Mention three occasions when Pip's 'expectations' are referred to.

Third stage

Chapter 40

Early next morning Pip stumbles over a stranger (Orlick) on the stairs but fails to trace him. Magwitch's assumed name is 'Provis' and Pip decides to call him his uncle. As he has come to stay, Pip also finds fresh clothes and quiet lodgings for him, and then calls on Jaggers to verify the news that has shattered his hopes. After five days Herbert returns and is let into the secret.

blood-'uns i.e. pedigree horse.
Botany Bay One of the earliest Australian penal colonies. (It was situated near the present city of Sydney.)
jack-knife A large clasp-knife for the pocket.
the Calendar i.e. the Newgate Calendar, a collection of notorious crimes from 1700 onwards, which was first published in 1774. Two updated series were brought out about 1826.
The imaginary student Frankenstein, who, in the story by Mary Shelley, published in 1818, galvanized a soulless monster made out of human fragments in the dissecting-room.

Chapter 41

Pip feels a great sense of relief once Provis is moved to new lodgings. Pip determines not to accept any more money from Provis but both he and Herbert are concerned that this course of action may lead the convict to give himself up. They decide that Pip will have to leave England as well.

Next morning they ask Provis to tell them about his past history.

Chapter 42

Magwitch relates the story of his criminal upbringing, his association with Compeyson, their trial for forgery (in which Compeyson was given a lighter sentence), his desire for revenge in the marshes, and his transportation. Compeyson is identified by Herbert as the man who had cheated Miss Havisham (in league with Arthur Havisham) by professing to be her lover.

Bridewells Bridewell, a prison in Blackfriars became so well-known that the name was synonymous with any prison.

Chapter 43

Before going abroad, Pip feels he must see Estella and Miss Havisham. At the Blue Boar he has an unpleasant encounter with Drummle, who makes no secret of the fact that he is to dine with Estella.

in a dust-coloured dress Cf. the watchman's description in Chapter 40.

Chapter 44

At Satis Pip upbraids Miss Havisham for her deception, points out the honesty of Matthew Pocket and Herbert as compared with her other relations, professes his love for Estella and, when told that she is to marry Drummle, declares in a passionate outburst how much she is a part of him. Back in London he is warned by a note from Wemmick not to return to his rooms.

making See note on 'doing', p.61.

Chapter 45

After a sleepless night in a lodging house, Pip sees Wemmick at Walworth, and is told that Magwitch's disappearance has led to enquiries. Pip is being watched, Compeyson is in London, so Wemmick felt it best for the convict to be moved downriver to the house in which Clara Barley and her father are living. He is advised to see Magwitch, take charge of his money and then wait in London.

Divinely Righteous From the Divine Right of the Stuart kings.
Argus A hundred-eyed watchman in Greek mythology.

Chapter 46

Pip manages to find the house and meets Clara. Magwitch, now called 'Mr Campbell', has softened considerably and agrees to leave England again with Pip, who, with Herbert, starts to row regularly on the Thames, to avoid suspicion when the day comes to board a steamer.

rope-walks The amount of rope needed for a sailing ship was amazing. In a clipper there would be about 8 km (5 miles) of cordage. In those days the rope was made by hand, with the help of a simple turning apparatus. The yarn-maker worked 'in the walk'. Hemp was tied round his body so that the ends of the fibres crossed each other behind his back. He drew out the ends of a few fibres with his left hand and fastened them to a hook; he then walked backwards away from the hook, laying out the hemp as he did so, while another man kept the hook revolving by means of a handle attached to a wheel governing the movement of the hook. The long line of fibres was thus twisted into a yarn.
bow-window Curved window (whereas a *bay*-window is rectangular).
Double Gloucester A kind of cheese.

Chapter 47

During weeks of waiting in suspense for a sign from Wemmick, Pip, who has refused to take any more of Magwitch's money, finds himself in financial difficulties. One evening, to relieve the tedium of constant rowing on the river, he visits the theatre and is startled to be told by Wopsle that the actor has seen, sitting behind Pip, the 'other convict' of the incident of the marshes. He writes a letter to Wemmick.

starlings Projections from a bridge at water-level to protect it against the force of the current.
Tartar A native of Tartary, an area including Turks, Cossacks etc., i.e. a wild man.
the last Census A playful reference to the number of actors on the stage.
Swab Clumsy fellow (naval slang).
I wrote it . . . and posted it In those days it would probably be delivered the same morning.

Chapter 48

At dinner with Wemmick at Mr Jaggers's rooms, Pip is given a note from Miss Havisham asking him to see her. Struck by the housekeeper's resemblance to Estella, Pip asks Wemmick on the way home, to tell him her story and hears that she once had a little girl.

at the Hummums See the first paragraph of Chapter 45.

As she withdrew her hands . . . arrested my attention Her hands and fingers are noted again. And lower, 'The action of her fingers was like the action of knitting' – Pip had often seen Estella knitting, e.g. the first paragraph of Chapter 44.

a stage-coach window Cf. Estella's arrival in London (Chapter 32).

not alone With Estella (Chapter 33).

identification in the theatre i.e. of Compeyson by Wopsle (Chapter 47).

over the broomstick i.e. it was a sham marriage.

Chapter 49

After giving Pip £900 to buy Herbert's partnership, Miss Havisham asks his forgiveness for the wrong she has done him and grovels on the floor in hysterical remorse. She explains that she originally intended to save Estella from her own fate; in response to his enquiry, she informs him that the girl was brought to her as an orphan about three years old by Jaggers. The recurrence as he is about to leave of a boyhood vision of Miss Havisham hanging from a beam causes him to return upstairs in time to see her on fire and to smother the flames. Leaving her unconscious in the charge of a surgeon, Pip spends the night at the old house before returning to London next morning.

A childish association See Chapter 8.

Chapter 50

Still suffering from burns, Pip is nursed by Herbert, who tells him how improved in manner Magwitch has become and also of Magwitch's relations with Molly, as related by the convict during Pip's absence. It is now clear that Magwitch is Estella's father.

some woman Molly, whose story is avoided by Magwitch in Chapter 42 and told by Wemmick in Chapter 48.

Revision questions on Chapters 40–50

1 Tell the story of Pip's whole connection with Miss Havisham.

2 What facts from the hidden past are revealed in these chapters?

3 In how many ways is Pip's mind troubled?

Chapter 51

At Little Britain Pip startles Jaggers by telling him who Estella's father is. When the lawyer seeks to put off further discussion, Pip appeals for his confidence in return and is told, with due caution, that Estella was taken from her mother, Molly the housekeeper, to be reared by Miss Havisham. Jaggers recommends that Estella's parentage should remain a secret.

a wiser head See Jaggers's remarks later in this chapter.
congestively Jointly.

Chapter 52

Pip learns that Clarriker proposes opening a branch-office in the East, of which Herbert is to take charge. A secretive note from Wemmick urges them to get Magwitch out of the country on the following Wednesday. They make enquiries about possible steamers, especially one due to sail for Hamburg. Herbert enlists the help of Startop, Pip secures passports and Magwitch is warned to be ready.

On the same day, Monday, an anonymous letter offers information about Pip's 'Uncle Provis' if he goes secretly to a rendezvous in the marshes. After enquiring about Miss Havisham at Satis, he has to listen to the story of his ingratitude to his 'benefactor', Pumblechook, from the landlord of another inn than the Blue Boar, and is filled with remorse for his very real ingratitude to Joe.

the land of the Arabian Nights i.e. the East, appearing to Herbert as a wonderland, as in the Arabic stories under this title.

Chapter 53

Making his way by moonlight across the desolate marshes, Pip reaches the appointed place, where he is seized by Orlick, tied to a ladder and given to understand he is to be killed and his body burnt in the lime kiln. From this fate he is rescued in the nick of time by Herbert, who had discovered Orlick's note at their rooms and with Trabb's Boy as guide had reached the sluice-house and heard Pip cry out. Tuesday is spent at the Temple, Pip's arm, having suffered when tied up by Orlick, being bathed to fit him for the next day's expedition.

a gun with a brass-bound stock See Chapter 29.
my words to Biddy See Chapter 35.

Chapter 54

Next morning, Herbert and Startop rowing and Pip steering, they pick up Magwitch, dressed as a pilot, and continue downriver past Gravesend. The night is spent at a lonely inn, where they hear of a mysterious boat hovering in the neighbourhood; in the moonlight Pip observes two men examining their boat. The following morning they are about to hail the Hamburg steamer when a police galley leaves the shore and pulls alongside, with a muffled figure in it. Magwitch is called on to surrender, but when hands are laid on him he pulls the cloak from the muffled figure and reveals Compeyson. The steamer runs down Pip's boat; the three young men are rescued, but the two convicts are once again at grips in the water. Compeyson is drowned and Magwitch taken into custody, together with the pocket-book containing his wealth. Pip is allowed to accompany the prisoner.

pea-coats Stout short overcoats of coarse woollen cloth, commonly worn then by sailors.
scullers Rowers.
respondent Answering back.
lightermen 'Lighters' were flat-bottomed barges for loading or unloading ships.
fenders Coils of rope swung over a ship's side to protect it against dock-sides, piers etc.
thowels Rowlocks.

Chapter 55

Magwitch is committed for trial in a month's time, and Jaggers offers no hope of recovering his wealth. Herbert offers Pip a clerkship in the new office, but the latter delays his answer for a couple of months.

Wemmick's explanation of their interception is that Compeyson had tricked them by letting it be known among his accomplices that he was away from London.

Pip is invited to Wemmick's wedding as best man, the ceremony being arranged by the habitually secretive bridegroom to appear as a series of coincidences. Mr Jaggers is not to be informed of the marriage.

Secondly His intention to propose to Biddy.
never looked . . . her grandpa A reference to Herbert's mother's preoccupation with titles.
Hymen A marriage song of the ancient Greeks; later personified as the god of marriage.

Chapter 56

In the prison infirmary Magwitch lies seriously injured (by the steamer's paddles) and getting weaker, but he is visited for a short time each day by Pip, who has transferred to him some of the romantic affection felt for Estella. At the sessions he is condemned to death with thirty-one others, after being singled out for special reprobation. Pip writes letters of appeal in vain. Just before Magwitch passes away (cheating the gallows), Pip tells him that his little daughter is a beautiful lady and that he loves her.

the two men . . . Temple to pray See Luke, 18,9–14.

Chapter 57

Now the long days of anxiety are over, a reaction sets in and Pip falls into a delirious fever, during which time he is summoned for debt but, because of his condition, he is not removed to a debtor's prison. After some weeks Pip comes out of his delirium and recognizes Joe at his bedside, the faithful blacksmith having nursed him all this time. Joe laboriously writes the news of Pip's recovery to Biddy and informs Pip that Miss Havisham is dead, having left £4,000 to Matthew Pocket and small sums to the other relations; also that Orlick is in prison for burgling Pumblechook's shop. Joe tactfully turns the conversation from Pip's penniless state and as the invalid gets stronger becomes less affectionate and more respectful. He leaves early one morning after settling Pip's debts. Three days later Pip sets out to explain everything to Joe and ask Biddy to marry him.

determine A legal term – come to an end, terminate.
coddleshell i.e. codicil.
to keep you and Tickler in sunders See Chapter 2.

Chapter 58

Pip finds Satis marked off in lots for sale and is patronizingly told by Pumblechook that his misfortune is the punishment of Providence for his ingratitude to his 'earliest benefactor'. He finds the schoolroom shut and the forge silent, but the parlour gay with flowers. Then, coming face to face with Joe and Biddy, he learns that it is their wedding day. He asks their forgiveness for his past conduct and bids them farewell.

Pip joins Herbert out East and shortly afterwards his friend is married to Clara on the death of her father. When Pip becomes a partner, Herbert is told by Clarriker the secret of his own partnership.

knock-knee i.e. crooked, slanting.

Chapter 59

Eleven years later, Pip returns to the forge and sees a small edition of himself in the kitchen. Paying a sentimental visit to the place where Satis stood he meets Estella, whose husband is dead after ill-treating her for years. She also is on a last visit to the old site. Changed in heart by her suffering, she asks if he still forgives her, and, in the calm light of the rising mists, they leave Satis for the last time, together.

the placid look . . . on earth Magwitch's last moments. See Chapter 56.

Revision questions on Chapters 51–9

1 Give a full account of Pip's association with Magwitch in these chapters.

2 Describe the plans for Magwitch's escape and explain their failure.

3 Pip's two greatest friends save his life on different occasions. Give an account in each case.

4 Tell the story of Pip in these last chapters as (*a*) Joe, (*b*) Herbert might have related it.

5 What is added to the story by the background of the River Thames in these chapters?

General questions

1 Indicate the appropriateness of the title *Great Expectations* by references to the plot of the novel.

2 How many kinds of expectations besides Pip's can you find in *Great Expectations*, and how far is each realized?

3 Give a brief account of three occasions in *Great Expectations* when somebody is taken by surprise.

4 Give an account of Pip's first meeting with the convict Magwitch on the marshes, bringing out its dramatic quality, and show how the rest of the novel develops from this scene.

5 Summarize the part played by Miss Havisham in the plot of *Great Expectations*.

6 Describe briefly (*a*) Pip's visit to Satis House after Miss Havisham's invitation has been brought to Pip in London by Joe, (*b*) his later visit after an invitation has been sent to Jaggers. How had Miss Havisham changed in the period between these two visits?

7 Describe the ways in which Pip keeps 'Provis' (Magwitch) safe in London and how he is helped to do so by his friends.

8 Show Dickens's power to hold the interest of his readers by giving an account of the drowning of Compeyson and the rescue of Magwitch from the Thames.

9 Comment on some of the letters in the story and the purposes with which they are written.

10 Using material taken from the novel comment on criminal law proceedings and punishments of that time.

11 Prove by reference to details mentioned in the story that it is set in the third decade of the nineteenth century.

12 Describe (*a*) a funeral, (*b*) a visit to the theatre, (*c*) a dame school, (*d*) a meal at an inn at the beginning of the nineteenth century, basing your answer on events in *Great Expectations*.

13 By reference to Pip's life at the blacksmith's and later in London analyse the effect upon him of becoming 'a gentleman of fortune'.

14 Describe Pip as seen by (*a*) Jaggers, (*b*) Trabb's boy, (*c*) Biddy, (*d*) Estella, at different times in the story.

15 'I was capable of almost any meanness towards Joe.' How far do you consider this to be a just comment?

16 Show what different features of Joe's character are shown in his relationship with (*a*) Pip, (*b*) Mrs Joe.

17 Which do you consider to have caused the greater harm to Pip, Miss Havisham or Magwitch? Refer closely to the novel.

18 Contrast the escaped convict with the returned transport.

19 Describe Pip's first impressions of Barnard's Inn and his first meeting there with Herbert Pocket, showing what features of the characters of Pip and Herbert can be discovered from this episode.

20 'It was the only good thing I had done, and the only completed thing I had done, since I was first apprised of my great expectations.' How far would you agree with Pip's estimate of his actions in this reference to his help of Herbert?

21 Illustrate Dickens's skill as a writer of humorous narrative from his account of life in Mr Matthew Pocket's home in Hammersmith.

22 By referring to relevant episodes in the novel contrast the home life of Mr and Mrs Pocket and that of John Wemmick and 'the aged P.' at Walworth.

23 What aspects of Mr Jaggers's character are revealed in (*a*) his meeting with Mr Wopsle at 'The Three Jolly Bargemen', (*b*) his first meeting with Pip in his office in Little Britain, (*c*) his meeting with Pip when Pip reveals the identity of Estella's father?

24 From *Great Expectations* illustrate (*a*) Pumblechook's hypocrisy, (*b*) Wemmick's caution, (*c*) Wopsle's ability as an actor.

25 Which characters in *Great Expectations* get (*a*) most enjoyment, (*b*) least enjoyment out of life? Illustrate your answer from the story.

26 How many characters receive (*a*) the reward, (*b*) the punishment they deserve? In what way?

27 Which characters show (*a*) greed for money, (*b*) indifference to it? On what occasions?

28 In which characters do you find it hardest to believe? Why?

29 What do you consider to be the most pathetic episode in *Great Expectations*? Give a brief account of it so as to bring out the source of its pathos.

30 Mention any one incident connected with *three* of the following places and give a brief account of it. The Temple, Covent Garden, the Blue Boar, Camberwell Green.

Pan study aids Titles published in the Brodie's Notes series

W. H. Auden Selected Poetry

Jane Austen Emma Mansfield Park Northanger Abbey Persuasion Pride and Prejudice

Anthologies of Poetry Ten Twentieth Century Poets The Metaphysical Poets The Poet's Tale

Samuel Beckett Waiting for Godot

Arnold Bennett The Old Wives' Tale

William Blake Songs of Innocence and Experience

Robert Bolt A Man for All Seasons

Harold Brighouse Hobson's Choice

Charlotte Brontë Jane Eyre

Emily Brontë Wuthering Heights

Robert Browning Selected Poetry

John Bunyan The Pilgrim's Progress

Geoffrey Chaucer (parallel texts editions) The Franklin's Tale The Knight's Tale The Miller's Tale The Nun's Priest's Tale The Pardoner's Tale Prologue to the Canterbury Tales The Wife of Bath's Tale

Richard Church Over the Bridge

John Clare Selected Poetry and Prose

Samuel Taylor Coleridge Selected Poetry and Prose

Wilkie Collins The Woman in White

William Congreve The Way of the World

Joseph Conrad The Nigger of the Narcissus & Youth The Secret Agent

Charles Dickens Bleak House David Copperfield Dombey and Son Great Expectations Hard Times Little Dorrit Oliver Twist Our Mutual Friend A Tale of Two Cities

Gerald Durrell My Family and Other Animals

George Eliot Middlemarch The Mill on the Floss Silas Marner

T. S. Eliot Murder in the Cathedral Selected Poems

J. G. Farrell The Siege of Krishnapur

Henry Fielding Joseph Andrews

F. Scott Fitzgerald The Great Gatsby

E. M. Forster Howards End A Passage to India
Where Angels Fear to Tread

William Golding Lord of the Flies The Spire

Oliver Goldsmith Two Plays of Goldsmith: She Stoops to Conquer; The Good Natured Man

Graham Greene Brighton Rock The Power and the Glory
The Quiet American

Thom Gunn and Ted Hughes Selected Poems

Thomas Hardy Chosen Poems of Thomas Hardy Far from the Madding Crowd Jude the Obscure The Mayor of Casterbridge
Return of the Native Tess of the D'Urbervilles The Trumpet-Major

L. P. Hartley The Go-Between The Shrimp and the Anemone

Joseph Heller Catch-22

Ernest Hemingway For Whom the Bell Tolls
The Old Man and the Sea

Barry Hines A Kestrel for a Knave

Gerard Manley Hopkins Poetry and Prose of Gerard Manley Hopkins

Aldous Huxley Brave New World

Henry James Washington Square

Ben Jonson The Alchemist Volpone

James Joyce A Portrait of the Artist as a Young Man

John Keats Selected Poems and Letters of John Keats

Ken Kesey One Flew Over the Cuckoo's Nest

Rudyard Kipling Kim

D. H. Lawrence The Rainbow Selected Tales Sons and Lovers

Harper Lee To Kill a Mocking-bird

Laurie Lee As I Walked out One Midsummer Morning
Cider with Rosie

Thomas Mann Death in Venice & Tonio Kröger

Christopher Marlowe Doctor Faustus Edward the Second

W. Somerset Maugham Of Human Bondage

Arthur Miller The Crucible Death of a Salesman

John Milton A Choice of Milton's Verse Comus and Samson Agonistes Paradise Lost, I, II

Sean O'Casey Juno and the Paycock The Shadow of a Gunman and The Plough and the Stars

George Orwell Animal Farm 1984

John Osborne Luther

Alexander Pope Selected Poetry

Siegfried Sassoon Memoirs of a Fox-Hunting Man

Peter Shaffer The Royal Hunt of the Sun

William Shakespeare Antony and Cleopatra As You Like It Coriolanus Hamlet Henry IV (Part I) Henry IV (Part II) Henry V Julius Caesar King Lear King Richard III Love's Labour's Lost Macbeth Measure for Measure The Merchant of Venice A Midsummer Night's Dream Much Ado about Nothing Othello Richard II Romeo and Juliet The Sonnets The Taming of the Shrew The Tempest Twelfth Night The Winter's Tale

G. B. Shaw Androcles and the Lion Arms and the Man Caesar and Cleopatra The Doctor's Dilemma Pygmalion Saint Joan

Richard Sheridan Plays of Sheridan: The Rivals; The Critic; The School for Scandal

John Steinbeck The Grapes of Wrath Of Mice and Men & The Pearl

Tom Stoppard Rosencrantz and Guildenstern are Dead

J. M. Synge The Playboy of the Western World

Jonathan Swift Gulliver's Travels

Alfred Tennyson Selected Poetry

William Thackeray Vanity Fair

Flora Thompson Lark Rise to Candleford

Dylan Thomas Under Milk Wood

Anthony Trollope Barchester Towers

Mark Twain Huckleberry Finn

Keith Waterhouse Billy Liar

Evelyn Waugh Decline and Fall Scoop

H. G. Wells The History of Mr Polly

John Webster The White Devil

Oscar Wilde The Importance of Being Earnest

Virginia Woolf To the Lighthouse

William Wordsworth The Prelude (Books 1, 2)

John Wyndham The Chrysalids

W. B. Yeats Selected Poetry

Australian Titles

George Johnston My Brother Jack

Thomas Keneally The Chant of Jimmy Blacksmith
Ray Lawler Summer of the Seventeenth Doll
Henry Lawson The Bush Undertaker & Selected Short Stories
Ronald McKie The Mango Tree
Kenneth Slessor Selected Poems
Ralph Stow The Merry-Go-Round in the Sea To the Islands
Patrick White The Tree of Man
David Williamson The Removalists